THE RIGH

THE RIGHTS OF WOMAN
The Essential Question-and-Answer Guide to Women's Legal Problems

Nicola Charles
(Wig)

Janice James
(Pen)

Illustrations by Frank Dickens

ARROW BOOKS

Arrow Books Limited
20 Vauxhall Bridge Road, London SW1V 2SA

An imprint of Random Century Group

London Melbourne Sydney Auckland
Johannesburg and agencies throughout
the world

First published by Arrow 1990

© Janice James and Nicola Charles 1990

This book is sold subject to the condition that it shall not, by way of trade or otherwise, be lent, resold, hired out, or otherwise circulated without the publisher's prior consent in any form of binding or cover other than that in which it is published and without a similar condition including this condition being imposed on the subsequent purchaser

Phototypeset by Input Typesetting Ltd, London

Printed and bound in Great Britain by
Courier International Ltd, Tiptree, Essex

ISBN 0 09 966230 2

CONTENTS

	Acknowledgments	6
	Authors' Preface	7
1	Shops and Services	9
2	Friends and Neighbours	25
3	Marriage and Divorce	35
4	Live-in Lovers	49
5	Children and Animals	55
6	Other People's Babies	68
7	Medical Matters	72
8	Money Matters	80
9	Danger – Women at Work!	97
10	Home Sweet Home	106
11	No Fixed Abode	120
	Appendix: Useful Addresses	131
	Making A Small Claim – It's No Big Deal	141
	Index	143

ACKNOWLEDGMENTS

The authors acknowledge and offer grateful thanks for the assistance provided by Derek Searle, Rosanna Bolton, John Stiles, Anna O'Connell and in particular Michael Clancy and Victor Levene.

Whilst every care has been taken to ensure that the information contained in this book is correct at the time of going to press, neither the authors nor the publishers warrant the accuracy thereof.

AUTHORS' PREFACE

Why a guide to the law aimed at women? Aren't we all, men and women, equal before the law so the same advice applies to us all? In theory, yes. But there are many areas in modern life where women need more specific help and encounter more problems – in the home, the high street, the workplace.

This handbook is intended to provide some answers to situations that can leave a woman (and maybe the man looking over her shoulder) stumped. It is not a detailed legal encyclopaedia but a guide to help you gain confidence and some insight into dealing with likely problems you may encounter in day-to-day life.

Where we have been able we have indicated how the law may differ in Scotland. (For legal procedures in Scotland and Northern Ireland, see also page 133.) We do stress, however, that wherever you live, if you have a serious legal problem, then you must seek professional and expert advice.

Some cases will call for specific information or guidelines tailored to your individual requirements. To assist you we have included a list of addresses and telephone numbers to put you on the first track in obtaining that guidance and advice.

Nicola Charles and Janice James

1. SHOPS AND SERVICES

Dressed in a little brief authority, saleswomen (and men) can seem positively draconian. If you buy something which you don't like or discover is faulty, or a workman does an unsatisfactory job, or a guarantee runs out the day after an appliance has gone wrong, what can you do?

Q: I bought a dress which I knew was too tight but the saleswoman was very persuasive and I told myself I'd lose five pounds and it would look fine. But I haven't and it doesn't. The nice saleswoman turned quite nasty. She says I can't have my money back but can have a credit note. I don't want one as I need a new dress and I need the cash to buy it elsewhere. Do I have to take the note?

A: Yes, you do. When you bought the dress, you were well aware of its shortcomings – or rather your own – and you are not entitled to reject it unless there is actually a fault with it. Some shops might even refuse a credit note and would be within their rights. So your new dress will have to come from the shop's available stock. Or you could go on a crash diet!

Q: I went to the hairdresser for blonde highlights. When I came out from the dryer, I was horrified. I'm not a punk so green streaks aren't for me! The hairdresser said he could do nothing for a few weeks for fear of damaging my hair but then he'd put it right. Can I claim anything for the time I've spent hiding indoors, afraid to go out for fear of being laughed at?

A: You are certainly entitled to claim for distress and anguish caused by your hairdresser's attempt to give you a new image. Damages awarded in cases like this are usually related to the particular effect the mistake has had upon the unfortunate victim. In principle, your claim would be met with sympathy although the damages awarded will rarely fully compensate for the misery you have undergone. Now you know what they mean when some people say that green is unlucky!

Q: I tried on a dress which was perfect for a special evening 'do' coming up. With no money on me I asked the shop to hold the dress until the following day when I could return and pay for it. The shop agreed, but when I went back as arranged, I discovered that the dress had been sold in the meantime by an assistant who did not know that it was being held. I was most upset as it was the only one in stock, but were the shop within their rights to do this?

A: If the shop had definitely agreed to sell the dress to you, then a contract of sale was created and, assuming you returned to pay for it within the stipulated time, the shop was actually in breach of the contract by selling it to someone else. You could have a claim against them for the extra cost (if any) of

having to purchase an alternative garment which might afford some 'redress' to you.

Q: I bought a freezer from a well-known electrical store and a few days after delivery the food began to thaw and a good deal of it was ruined. The freezer was obviously faulty and the store replaced it with another. However, when I claimed for the costs of the ruined food the store eventually sent me a cheque for the full amount but wrote that they were making payment as 'goodwill' and that this was in full and final settlement of any further claims I might have. I am now concerned that in accepting the cheque I will not be able to claim if my replacement freezer goes wrong.

A: Rest assured. If any fault develops in your new freezer, your rights are unaffected by the previous settlement, which related only to your ruined food and not to any claim which might arise for the replacement freezer. By the way, from what you have said, you were entitled to that cheque whether sent with 'goodwill' or not.

Q: I've been to see a solicitor about a case I wish to bring against my former employers. His advice was totally negative although I know I have a strong case and former colleagues are prepared to back me. He stirred himself once to talk vaguely about settling out of court, which I don't want to do as the principle is as important to me as the money. Would it be all right to go to another solicitor and, if so, do I have to pay the first man the full fee?

A: You are always entitled to change your solicitor – particularly if you feel less than confident as to the advice or attention you are getting. However, the first solicitor will generally be entitled to keep hold of the papers entrusted to him by you, and all documents relating to your case, until he has been paid. So if

you cannot manage without them, you will have to pay. You can challenge his bill if you believe it to be too high for the amount of work done, by asking for what is called a 'taxation', which is an assessment of his charges made independently by a court officer. But unless you can show his conduct amounted to incompetence you will almost certainly have to pay him something.

One word of caution – principles can turn out to be very expensive where litigation is concerned.

Q: Since in every case brought, there's a lawyer who wins and one who doesn't, how do I find a good lawyer? I've heard some real horror stories!

A: Well, this question really follows on from the one above. And let us say straight away that the lawyer who loses a case may not necessarily be the bad guy, just the one who came second! There are many other people and factors involved when you embark on legal proceedings. Word of mouth is one way of getting a good lawyer. And the Law Society can provide a list of solicitors in your area. You can write to The Law Society, 113 Chancery Lane, London WC2 1PA, or in Scotland, The Law Society of Scotland, 26–28 Drumsheugh Gardens, Edinburgh EH3 7YR.

Q: I was on my way out of the supermarket when I was stopped by a man who looked like the manager. He asked to see my bag, which he examined most carefully. Quite a few people I know saw me and it was terribly embarrassing. I hadn't taken anything I hadn't paid for, so that was that. But the man barely apologised and I feel very angry. I feel as though my neighbours are looking at me and saying I'm a thief. Do I have any case for redress against the store?

A: Apart from a strong letter of protest to the store

for the lack of apology, there is really nothing else you can do. You were asked and consented to have your bag searched and therefore there is no question of what is called 'false imprisonment'. You were not accused falsely of any theft, and so no defamation arises – nor were you prosecuted wrongly and so there was no malicious prosecution. Whilst understanding your embarrassment, the man at the store was just doing his job – perhaps overzealously and without the appropriate manners to admit his wrong suspicions. Hopefully you will find that any interest your neighbours might have in your discomfort will wane when they find more interesting and genuine matters to concern themselves about.

Q: My mother arranged for a local upholsterer to repair and recover an antique chair. The work was estimated to take six weeks but many months have gone by and my mother is being fobbed off with one excuse after the other as to why the chair is not ready. She is now rather worried as the chair is quite valuable and the upholsterer refuses even to answer her calls or letters. What should she do?

A: Your mother must deliver an ultimatum in writing to the upholsterer, demanding her chair by a specified date. If this brings no result we suggest that she take advice with a view to legal proceedings. The upholsterer is either recklessly inefficient or a crook, and whichever it is, the time has come to claim against him for the return of the chair or its value, plus damages for the loss of use of the chair.

Q: My mother, who is an avid knitter, wanted to buy a knitting pattern in a local shop the other day but the shopkeeper refused to sell her the pattern unless she also bought the wool to go with it. Could my mother have insisted on purchasing the pattern without the wool?

A: Afraid not. When anyone goes into a shop, a contract is formed only when the shopkeeper agrees to sell to the customer. The shopkeeper can therefore refuse to sell his goods or impose terms for the sale as he wishes. In your mother's case it seems that the shopkeeper was within his rights, but he's probably lost a good customer through lack of goodwill.

Q: Do I have any remedy against a builder who now refuses to carry out work at the price agreed on his quotation? He claims that he costed the work below its value and insists that I agree to an increase before he will undertake the job.

A: The builder is in breach of contract by insisting on an increase, and whilst you cannot force him to carry out the job at the original price agreed, you are entitled to employ another builder to do the work to the same standard. However, if you now have to pay more for the work, you can look to the original builder to compensate you for the difference.

Q: Having recently moved into my new house I needed a kitchen table which I ordered from a local department store and they promised to deliver it on the following Wednesday. They could not give a definite time of delivery but said it would be between 9 a.m. and 1 p.m. I duly took time off work but the table did not appear. When I rang the store to complain, they said the delivery men had arrived at 1.05 p.m. to find nobody at home. We then arranged another delivery date and again I took the morning off work and again there was no sign of the table. This time 'the van had broken down' and we arranged yet another date. The table was eventually delivered, but I lost three mornings' pay as I am a freelance designer. Can I claim any costs from the store?

A: However infuriating, it is doubtful that you would

have a claim. It seems that you were given the dubious benefit of 'free' delivery when you made your purchase. Such benefit is likely to be in the nature of a side arrangement for which no separate payment was made, and therefore a claim is unlikely to succeed. You would be clearly in a stronger position if the delivery had been an express term of the contract to purchase the table, or if you had to pay the store to deliver the goods.

Q: I am a pensioner and rely heavily on my television for entertainment. Recently it has started playing up and a friend gave me the name of a TV repairman who works from home. He took my television away, but within a few days of having it back it went wrong again. Since then I have had to call him out twice more and each time he has taken the TV away to repair – and bills so far have amounted to £150. I realise that I should not have used a potential 'cowboy' operator, but can I claim back any of the money I have paid out to him, as I am sure he is taking me for an expensive ride?

A: You could well have a claim for the return of *all* your money. If you paid for repairs which were plainly not done, or were so inept as to render the television no better than before, then you are entitled to recover the cost of these so-called repairs, and the 'small claims' procedure through your local county or sheriff's court would appear to be your best bet to attempt to get your money back.

Q: I was given a credit note for returned goods but when I attempted to make a purchase in the shop for half of the value of the note, the manager informed me that I had to spend the whole lot in one go and could receive no change, nor a further note if I failed to do so. I protested, but under pressure I eventually bought some goods I didn't really want just to use up the note. Could I have insisted on spending as much or as little as I pleased on the credit note at one time?

A: If, when you first exchanged the goods, you were not entitled to a refund but the shop exercised goodwill in taking them back and giving you a credit note, then you take the note subject to any condition imposed by the shop. It may be argued that this is true even if you were entitled to a refund but elected instead to take credit. So it is likely that you would only be able to 'spend' the note as the shop directed. This is why it is always better to get a refund when you are entitled to one.

Q: My parents run a newsagent's and stationer's, and a customer has defaulted on a long-running account, leaving a debt of over £100 on stationery supplies. He admits the debt but refuses to pay the money, saying that it was his company's liability and the company has gone into liquidation. My parents can ill afford to meet this deficit and wonder if they do have a claim against him as the account was in his name and, although he did pay some bills on a company cheque, they never realised they were dealing with a company.

A: Oh dear – your parents are the victims of an all too common dodge by unscrupulous debtors. If they were led to believe that they were supplying an individual at all times and the account was in a personal name as you say, then there is every reason to suppose that they can indeed go against their customer for their money in spite of what he says. The fact that a company cheque was sometimes used to pay bills ought to make no difference whatsoever and may merely indicate that the customer chose to use a company bank account to pay his own bills.

Q: I joined a postal book club and, after ordering and

paying for the required number of books, I exercised my rights and wrote to the club cancelling my membership. Since then I have regularly received a book every month and, despite further letters and phone calls, they keep coming. The books are still wrapped, unread and unwanted, and I am now getting demands for payment. Help!

A: Help is at hand! Your choice of action is as follows: either calmly write and inform the club that the books were neither ordered nor wanted and await collection by them; *or* simply pop them back into the post with 'return to sender' written on the package and without postage. You are not obliged to go to any expense or trouble but neither are you entitled simply to keep the books, or throw or give them away – however tempted you may be.

Q: Our house was advertised for sale by local estate agents but then we changed our minds about wanting to sell and withdrew our instructions. Some weeks later we were approached by a couple who had seen the advertisement, and they are very keen to buy. If, after all, we do go ahead, would we have to pay the agents, who are no longer acting for us and really did very little to earn their percentage?

A: We are forced to tell you that you are liable to pay the agents their commission since it was their advertising which secured your purchasers. We should add that estate agents always seem to have an uncanny knack of finding out about purchasers even when they have ceased acting for you, so you might as well come clean and perhaps see if you can negotiate with the agents on what is, for them, an unexpected windfall if the sale goes through.

Q: I took an expensive silk shirt to the dry cleaner's and when I collected it I was horrified to find that it had a huge scorch mark in the front where none had been before. It was ruined. When I complained, the manager of the shop casually pointed to a small sign above the counter which stated that all items were cleaned at the customer's risk. Can this be right? Have I any basis to claim?

A: No to your first question. Yes to your second. Frankly, had the sign been emblazoned in neon lights it would not help the shop one bit. There is an Act of Parliament called the Unfair Contract Terms Act 1977 which was designed to protect customers from shops which attempt to avoid liability by signs such as these. Put your complaint in writing to the manager, setting out all the facts and claiming compensation. If that doesn't do the trick, go to your local county or sheriff's court and take out a summons under the 'small claims' jurisdiction. From what you say you seem to have a valid claim to pursue. Go ahead!

Q: My boyfriend and I attended a furniture exhibition and ordered a three-piece suite for our flat from one of the stands. We paid a deposit and the salesman told us to expect delivery in six to eight weeks. That was *six months ago*! We have telephoned and chased them up but all we are told is that the furniture is on the way, with apologies for the delay. Frankly, we are fed up waiting and, although we really wanted that furniture, we have now seen a suite we like almost as much in a local store. Can we cancel and get our money back?

A: We admire your patience in waiting this long! Since you would still like to have this suite, write to the firm and inform them that as they are well over their promised delivery time, you will now put a time limit on the contract of, say, two weeks, failing which the order will be cancelled and you will expect the immediate return of your deposit. It never ceases to amaze us how quickly firms react to such letters, suddenly able to effect immediate delivery! However, if neither the furniture nor the deposit is forthcoming, you can at least seek the return of your money by issuing a summons in your local county court or by applying to the sheriff's court in Scotland.

Q: We bought a TV set from a branch of high street electrical goods retailers. The remote control went wrong after a short time and the shop agreed to repair it. That was three months ago! We have constantly been in touch with the shop but we are just told that repairs are taking longer than anticipated. We haven't been able to use the set and we still do not know when to expect the control back. Is there anything we can do?

A: It is difficult to understand why the shop did not supply you with a replacement control immediately! At the very least they should by now have either repaired or replaced yours. You must go in and demand action and, furthermore, you could be able to claim damages for the period that the set has been out of use – equivalent to the cost of hiring an alternative TV. A visit followed by a strong letter ought to get this shop 'switched on' for action to satisfy you.

Q: We treated my daughter to driving lessons at the local driving school for her birthday. We were told to pay the driving instructor for the course on the first lesson and we gave him a cheque. However, at his request we left the 'payee' blank for him to fill in the 'correct' account name. He gave us a card with the lessons listed on it. After five lessons I was informed by the driving school that the instructor had been arrested for theft of driving school funds which he paid into his own account, and the school are now refusing to give my daughter the lessons due unless we pay over again for them – nor will they refund any monies paid. Can they do this? They say they are not liable for their dishonest employee.

A: The driving school is wrong. On their instructions you paid their employee, who had apparent authority to accept payment on the school's behalf. Whether cheque or cash was stolen by him, it was stolen from his employers and not from you. Therefore the driving school must bear the consequences of their crooked employee, and if they refuse to give your daughter the lessons still due, or the balance of your money for these lessons, you can seek reimbursement through the small claims procedure in your local county or sheriff's court.

Q: A year ago, we purchased a violin for our son from reputable suppliers of musical instruments at a cost of nearly £500. From the start, our son had problems in tuning and six months ago the wood split. The suppliers refused to replace it but carried out repairs and assured us it was as new. However, the violin is still unsatisfactory and it looks as if we are going to have to purchase another. Have we any remedy against the suppliers?

A: If the violin was indeed an inferior instrument then you could well be entitled to recoup at least the difference between what you paid and what it was actually worth. You might even be entitled to the full cost price back if you could show that the quality of the instrument was expressly misrepresented to you. In order to recover anything, you would undoubtedly need an expert's opinion to state that the violin was unfit for the purpose for which it was required.

Q: I recently bought a baby's dungaree set which shrank after one wash although I had followed the washing instructions. When I returned them to the shop, the manager refused to change them because I had washed them

SHOPS AND SERVICES

and he could not have them replaced by the manufacturer. They were expensive and had only been worn once, but is there really nothing I can do?

A: You can go straight back to the shop and insist on your money back. The goods proved to be deficient and the shopkeeper is legally bound to provide you with a refund regardless of the manufacturer's attitude. Your contract is with the shopkeeper.

Q: My daughter purchased a jump suit from a stall at our local market. She wore it once, and when she washed it according to the instructions, it shrank and the colours ran. She returned it to the stall holder, who refused to give her the money back. He offered an exchange but she does not want this. Can she insist on her money back?

A: Stall holders are in no different position from shop owners. If the goods are defective then your daughter is entitled to her money back and can (and should) refuse to be fobbed off with an exchange. In view of the man's attitude we recommend you to report the matter to the local market inspector's office and even to the appropriate section of the local authority – both of whom may have some say in his licence to operate the stall. Perhaps if you tell him this is your intention, he'll see things differently!

Q: I booked a winter holiday in Tenerife but, just a few days before I was due to go, my travel agent phoned and said we had to take a different flight from a different airport. This meant that a much more expensive train journey was involved. Can I charge the travel agent for the extra expense involved?

A: Generally speaking, the travel agent acts on your behalf when he books your holiday and cannot be held accountable to you for any extras you might be called upon to pay. Here you need to investigate the precise circumstances of the change in itinerary and also check the conditions of booking (the inevitable small print). If by 'travel agent' you really mean the tour operator, then you may well be in a different position. The brochure or travel details upon which you relied to book the holiday must be looked at very carefully.

Q: I had an accident in 1979. A writ was issued for court proceedings in 1982 and the case has been prepared but no date has yet been given for the trial to be held. I've been in contact with my solicitors but cannot get satisfaction from them and my patience is exhausted. Is there any reason why I should not go to another solicitor even though I am supported by legal aid? Also, how do I know if my legal aid is still valid?

A: It seems a pity that your case cannot now be heard without going to the trouble of changing your solicitors, but if your present solicitors seem reluctant to keep you fully informed as to the progress of your case, there is nothing to prevent you from instructing a new firm of solicitors and your file will be passed to them.

Before taking this step, we would advise you to insist upon an appointment with your present solicitors to air your concerns fully and to find out about your legal aid position, and then you can decide whether to stay where you are or change to a new firm.

Q: My friend and I went for a meal in a rather expensive restaurant. It was a treat to ourselves to celebrate my friend getting a new job. They put us at a table hidden away in a corner and, frankly, the service was terrible and the food indifferent. We complained but received no apologies. If they didn't want women dining alone then they shouldn't have accepted us. What I want to know is whether we would have been within our rights to walk out without paying the bill? We didn't want to cause a scene but paid and left. And the infuriating thing was that the service was included so we couldn't even show our anger by withholding a tip.

A: Why do we so often suffer in silence, seethe and aggravate ourselves later?

If you get a rotten table and awful service and food, don't be afraid of demanding better *there and then* and if it is not forthcoming, don't put up with it while grumbling under your breath. You can refuse to sit at the table, refuse to accept the food and walk out without paying.

On the other hand, if, ghastly though your meal is, you accept both food and service, you are liable to pay for it in full – although it could be worth your while to speak to the management and argue for a discount.

You do have to pay service charges if they are clearly printed on the menu or otherwise brought to your attention before you order. Where service is charged, this must now be included in the cost of the meal, and the restaurant which fails to do so, commits an offence. Service charges cannot now be simply tacked on to the bill at the end of the meal. If you are disgruntled with the service, you are at liberty then to dispute them. If you refuse to pay, you should leave your name and address in case the restaurant wishes to pursue you by legal action for these charges – which is unlikely. Even if you did know of the service charge prior to ordering, you can still complain and argue for a reduction, but you are not entitled simply to refuse to pay and walk out. If you do walk out and refuse to pay either for food or service which the restaurant has provided you may well be committing a criminal offence under the

Theft Act 1978, or, in Scotland, under the common law of theft.

2. FRIENDS AND NEIGHBOURS

At least with enemies you know where you stand. Friends and neighbours can be tricky because problems with them may cause embarrassment and regret as well as trouble.

Q: A young couple has just moved into the flat next door. They are both unemployed and I'm sorry for them. But they do have their friends round and play loud music well into the early hours as they sleep late. We have to get up early for work and we're just so terribly tired. We've tried remonstrating with them and things are all right for a few days but then it starts again. Last time I mentioned it to the wife, she became very abusive. It was quite frightening. What can I do to stop it without getting involved in court proceedings which might make life intolerable?

A: Life seems pretty intolerable for you already, and as complaining has had little effect, you may well end up having to seek a court injunction or interdict in Scotland to restrict your neighbours' hours of play. If the noise is very loud, an approach, first, to your local authority might help. An official armed with a noise meter might be able to enforce a reduction in volume if the music amounts to noise pollution.

Q: I lent my friend a very special and expensive blouse. The waiter spilled soup on it and it left a nasty stain. She had it cleaned but the stain hasn't completely come out. She can't afford to replace it as it did cost a lot, but neither can I. Is there anything I can do? Should the hotel pay up? I'm afraid my friend and I are barely on speaking terms now.

A: To ensure long-lasting friendships, don't sell your car to a friend and don't lend good clothes! However, in this case, the hotel ought certainly to pay up. Waiters are not expected to throw things over guests except in comedy sketches and the hotel management is liable to you for the negligence of its staff.

Q: We have fallen out with our next-door neighbour, who took exception to my husband cutting back his overhanging cherry trees even though the trees nearly reached our lounge window. Now we want to widen our drive, but about three years ago the same neighbour planted some fir trees on our side of the drive which are in the way of the area to be widened. What advice do you have?

A: Are you ready for the unpopular neighbour of the year award? Right – then get to work and pull up those trees which are trespassing on your land and have no right to be there. Nor indeed was your husband doing more than properly exercising his entitlement in cutting back the cherry trees. By overhanging your garden they had become a legal 'nuisance'.

Q: My daughter's neighbour is claiming the costs of damage to her back door which she says was caused by my daughter's labrador. The neighbour has a bitch who was in season when a number of dogs entered her garden through a hole in the back wall, although the neighbour insists that only my daughter's dog was seen. Does my daughter have to pay for this damage? The neighbour is threatening court action.

A: If your daughter's dog was indeed responsible for the damage to the door, then she could well be held liable for the costs of repair if her dog was unrestrained and she was aware that it was likely to enter the neighbour's garden when the next-door dog was in season and cause the sort of damage complained of. However, the neighbour has first to prove that the labrador was the responsible 'party' and that it was not one of the other dogs whose owner she is unable to identify.

Q: My pet rabbit was savaged by a dog which ran into my garden whilst it was out walking with its owner in the nearby park. My pet had to be put down due to its injuries and I am most upset – particularly as the dog's owner merely called off his dog and walked away. Can I do anything, even though I know it won't bring my rabbit back?

A: This insensitive dog owner could be liable to you for the value of your pet and even, perhaps, your distress if it could be shown that the dog was likely to cause injury or damage by reason of its breed or training. The fact that the dog was unrestrained and permitted to trespass on to your property adds weight to your claim. You, or the police on your behalf, might also succeed in obtaining a control order on the dog by a summons in the magistrates' court, or an interdict in the sheriff's court in Scotland.

Q: Recently our next-door neighbours moved house and

in their place a single young man moved in. Every time he goes out he reverses his car over part of our front lawn, which is now looking decidedly the worse for wear. We have placed a plastic bollard near the spot and dropped a polite note through his letterbox asking him to drive more carefully, but so far nothing has changed. What legal steps, if any, can we take to let him know we mean business?

A: Your thoroughly inconsiderate neighbour commits a trespass every time his car comes into contact with any part of your property. You are entitled to obtain a court order against him to prevent the trespass from continuing and you can claim damages for the 'wear and tear' to your lawn. A firm letter from you or, better still, a solicitor on your behalf, ought to make him sit up and finally take notice of what is in store unless he mends his ways.

Q: My neighbours are pensioners, but they have made our lives almost unbearable by being vindictive and spiteful towards me and my family. We had to get rid of our dog because our neighbour kept letting him out and complained (falsely) that our dog had damaged his fence. Their son came round and threatened us and we have had visits from the social services after 'anonymous' calls that we were abusing our children. It is one thing after another and we wish we could stop them somehow.

A: This is not easy for you because complaints about insidious nastiness can sometimes be made to sound feeble when pulled to pieces in court proceedings. If, however, you can show that your neighbours' behaviour amounts to harassment, then you might well be able to get a court order against them, especially if you could show that the ghastly son was acting with his parents' knowledge and consent. The threats could, in any event, amount to a criminal offence for which you would be entitled to involve the police. We strongly advise you to take formal legal advice before embarking on any court action in this distressing situation.

Q: Our neighbour has cut down a large tree in his garden and allowed it to fall on our fence, damaging it and two shrubs in our garden. He has refused to pay for the damage or put it right. We would like to recover compensation, but as our claim is only £50 we want to know the most economical way to go about this.

A: The best thing is to take proceedings in the 'small claims court' by going along to your local county or sheriff's court. The procedure is quite straightforward and, bearing in mind how much compensation you seek, the costs to you of issuing and pursuing the claim should be very modest indeed.

Q: My neighbour has been away for several weeks and I thought they had returned early as I heard movements in the house. However, a few days ago I realised that the house had been taken over by squatters. The police say they cannot act. Is there anything I can do to get these people out before my neighbours return, and if not, what remedy will my neighbours have? They will be horrified.

A: You are clearly a caring friend as well as a good neighbour, but unfortunately that will not give you any rights to take action against these squatters. When your neighbours return and have recovered from their initial shock, they will be able to seek immediate relief from the courts by taking out proceedings to regain their property. It is not necessary for you or them to find out the precise identity of the squatters. Once a court order is obtained the squatters can then be evicted, by bailiffs or sheriff officers if necessary.

Q: My neighbour has a Russian vine which grows very fast and which he never bothers to cut back. Over the past few months it has grown through his fence and is now taking over my garden too. Three times I have had to cut it back on my side of the fence. Can I force my neighbour to do this for me? Or better still, can I make him take down the vine altogether?

A: Both the vine and the dispute between you and your neighbour seem to be fast growing. The growth into your garden is an encroachment which you are perfectly entitled to deal with as you have already done. Unfortunately, you cannot force your neighbour to be co-operative nor can you force him to remove the vine altogether. However, if you are seriously bothered by this state of affairs, you can work out the costs to you, in time and effort, of this pruning operation and charge it up to him, suing if necessary through the local county or sheriff's court. He ought to get the message by then – but don't ever ask to borrow his lawn mower!

Q: My mother lives in a semi-detached house in a residential road. Next door the property is tenanted by a family whose son has recently been operating a disco in the downstairs room adjacent to my mother's lounge. The noise going on to the small hours every night is making my mother's life a misery – not only is it the loud music but the coming and going of cars and people. Her polite requests that the activity be limited has been met with abuse. Can she take any action short of starting court proceedings?

A: She can and should report the matter without delay to the housing or planning department of her local authority. Her neighbours are almost certainly in breach of the planning regulations governing the use of residential property and it is a safe bet that

they have started the disco without the necessary planning permission to carry on such an activity. If they had applied for this, your mother would most certainly have known. The local authority have extensive powers to stop this activity and she should find them helpful and sympathetic. Only in the last resort should court proceedings be necessary to get an order against her inconsiderate neighbours.

Q: For some years now I have picked the apples from the overhanging branches of the next-door tree and made pies which my family enjoy. This summer, however, new neighbours moved in and we became quite friendly, until the day when we had a heated exchange about my picking the apples, which they objected to. I am rather upset by this, but surely it can't be reasonable for them to make such a fuss as, after all, the apples do overhang our garden and my husband says I must be entitled to pick them.

A: No comment as to whether your neighbours are reasonable but, sorry, your husband is wrong. The apples on the tree remain your neighbours' property – you are entitled only to cut back the overhanging branches if you are so minded. We suggest that you restore good relations by offering to make one of your delicious pies for your neighbours in exchange for the apples and avoid, thereby, any more 'fruity' encounters in the garden.

Q: My parents live close to a youth club and on several occasions damage has been caused to their car and neighbours' cars by the people attending the youth club. They have contacted the police and numerous councillors to try and get the club closed but to no avail. Please have you any suggestions as to what action they can take next?

A: It looks as if the only course open to your parents and their neighbours is to try to pressurise the local authority into imposing a change of user of the premises so that the club can no longer operate. If the premises are licensed they may be able to raise sufficient objections to the renewal of this licence when it is due. Regrettably, there seems no further remedy available as there is no liability on the part of the club for damage caused on the public highway – unless the persons responsible for the damage were acting on behalf of the club.

Q: An elderly neighbour has just bought a Rottweiler dog. He appears to have little control over it and it's only by a miracle that one of the children on the estate wasn't bitten last week. I think it's only time before he does attack someone and inflict real harm. I feel sorry for the old man because his flat has been broken into a few times but I'm worried about letting my children go out to play. Is there anything we can do to avert the danger?

A: **Some people still operate under the old maxim that says 'Every dog is entitled to one bite!' But in the modern world the law acts to protect persons who are placed in danger by dangerous animals.**

Nobody is entitled to have a guard dog at a dwelling unless there is a handler who is properly able to control the dog, which must not be allowed to roam freely about. Your neighbour may well be committing a criminal offence under the Guard Dogs Act 1975 and you should approach your local police.

Any dog which is dangerous and not kept under proper control can be made the subject of a control order in the magistrates' court (not Scotland). The owner will be fined for every day that he fails to comply with the order. Indeed, if the dog is proved to be dangerous and causes injury, the court can order it to be destroyed.

In the first place, you should have a chat with your neighbour and explain your fears. Hopefully he will understand and act upon them without the need for you to go further.

Q: I was telephoned by a newspaper recently for my comments on a neighbour who is involved in a criminal case. He was very easy to talk to and I'm afraid I rambled on a bit. As I was a bit worried about what I might have said, I rang him and he repeated some of the things I was supposed to have said. I asked him not to use a few of them as, on reflection, I didn't mean what I'd said. He became quite officious and said that not only was he going to use them but he had recorded our entire conversation. I really have two questions. Can a journalist quote what you've said (and I'm sure I said what he says I did) even though you've changed your mind? And, since he didn't tell me he was taping our conversation, is it legal to use it?

A: If you volunteer information to a journalist – knowing he is a journalist – then you must expect to see your words in print! Discretion is always the better part of friendliness where the demon press is concerned and so, yes, the journalist can use the information he has been given. As to whether a conversation can be recorded when one party knows nothing of the recording device, generally anything that can be heard by one's ear can be recorded electronically quite legally, and thus the journalist is entitled to publish what he recorded since you were aware of his status when you spoke to him.

Q: I had an affair with a pop star who gave a series of concerts in our town last year. I was very thrilled about it and wrote letters with all the details to my friend who had gone to work in London. Now she tells me that she has been offered a large sum of money by a newspaper to talk about the singer and she intends using extracts from my letters. Can she do this?

A: You know what they say: Do right and fear no man; don't write and fear no woman!

Seriously, you let yourself in for this one. Generally speaking, as long as information is true there is no bar on its publication, but in this instance the information was intended only for your so-called friend's consumption.

Any use of the information in the letters by her could be seen as a breach of confidentiality and the court might well agree to put a stop to the publication of any material or information extracted from your letters. Furthermore, any attempt by your 'friend' to quote directly from your letters could certainly be stopped since the copyright belongs to you. The publication of any part of the letters would be actionable as a breach of copyright and you could certainly prevent this by way of a court injunction. Next time, if you feel the urge to put pen to paper – try a diary and lock it away!

3. MARRIAGE AND DIVORCE

United we stand, divorced we often fall out. It's a sad fact that couples who were once in love and wanted to be with each other for ever are often involved in the most acrimonious recriminations when the relationship starts to falter.

In the first flush of romance, it is unthinkable that a marriage might fail so people tend not to make plans for this contingency. There's a lot to be said for arranged marriages! Everyone should think ahead, compare their attitudes to children and how they would work out their finances, property and custody of any children in the event of a divorce. Those of you who have been sensible enough to do all this can pass to the next chapter.

Q: We have been divorced for three years and our seven-year-old son lives with me. He goes to the local, very good, state school and is happy there. Now my ex-husband is saying he wants Tom to go to his old school where the boys in his family have been for four generations. I don't want Tom to go away to school. Also, I believe in state education (one of the bones of contention between my husband and me). My ex-husband says he will fight me on this and that he will win because he has the right to decide and pay for his child's education. Is this so?

A: If your husband has joint custody rights over Tom, then, strictly speaking, he has *as much* say as you – but not more – about his son's education. If you have been awarded sole custody, then you probably have more right than he. In either case, an issue like this would have to be the subject of court hearings, and while Tom's interest and happiness will be of paramount importance, you have to be on guard that a court might regard his interest as being the fifth generation at the old school. If, however, it means his being at boarding school, as you indicate, your ex might have a tougher fight on his hands.

Q: My marriage is a very unhappy one. We have very little money, which doesn't help, and my husband drinks heavily. He forces his sexual attentions on me and I dread the thought of his coming home at night. I'd like to get away but he says he'd follow me and never let me go. My friend says I can accuse him of rape and get a divorce. Is this true? Even if I did, though, I'd be afraid of his catching up with me.

A: You do not need to accuse your husband of rape to get a divorce. However, your husband's general behaviour can certainly amount to unreasonable conduct, which can be the basis of a divorce petition. Pending a divorce, and even afterwards, you would be entitled to seek the protection of the court if you feared your husband's threats and advances. You do this by obtaining an injunction restraining him from any molestation of you whatsoever. In England you would need an injunction or a legal separation order for your husband's conduct to be considered as rape although in Scotland it seems that a rape charge is possible against a husband actually and lawfully living with his wife.

Q: My husband has left me and I've just discovered that he's wiped out the contents of our joint account. It contained a lot of money as we both have high disposable incomes and spend a lot. Can I get my share back?

A: You can sue your husband for the return of your share of the account since he is not entitled to spend your part of the money without accounting to you for it. However, this could cost more money. If you can frighten him with this information into repaying what he owes, so much the better.

Q: I love everything about my fiancé. There's just one thing wrong with him. I have a very nice surname and his is horrible. Is it possible for the man to take his wife's name when they marry instead of the other way round?

A: Only one thing wrong with him? My goodness, you're a lucky girl! Now, as to that one wrong thing. The adoption by a wife of her husband's name is a long-accepted convention, but there is absolutely nothing to stop you turning that convention round and have your husband adopt and be known by your surname. He can call himself what he likes but if he wishes to change his name formally to yours, he can do so by deed poll or, in Scotland, by simply advertising the fact.

Q: I would like to know whether my husband has the right to half the value of our house when he has paid only towards the mortgage and nothing else. We are now separated and the house has been sold and I have been rehoused by the council because I am disabled. All I have to live on is a small income from an investment I made with money from a previous divorce settlement. My husband, on the other hand, has his own business and has not maintained either me or our two children who were still at school when we parted.

A: If the house was in joint names, your husband could well be entitled to receive his half-share of the property. But if your case comes before the court after a divorce, the result depends, in the long run, on the needs and assets of each party. The fact that your husband has never maintained you will be an important consideration when dealing with the distribution of the property.

Q: Following my divorce settlement, I agreed to buy out my ex-husband's share in our house. I had six months to find the capital, which I eventually did although delays meant that I was three months over the time limit before my ex-husband was paid out. He has responded by deducting maintenance payments due to our son for those three months, claiming that he has lost the equivalent interest on the money that was due to him for that period. Can and should I claim the money back from him? I get no maintenance for myself.

A: Your ex-husband had no right to deduct maintenance due to your son and if you were to claim it back, the court would undoubtedly enforce the full maintenance against him. However, if you bring proceedings you do risk facing a claim from your husband for the interest to which he might well be found entitled. You could therefore find that your gain on the one hand is offset by your loss on the other. Whether your claim is a worthwhile exercise depends upon whether your ex-husband brings his cross-claim, and his mean and small-minded conduct to date makes this more rather than less likely.

MARRIAGE AND DIVORCE

Q: I was a widow with two children (now 25 and 24, married with children of their own) when I met my present husband six years ago. We live in the house my first husband left me but my husband pays all the bills and has bought a small cottage in the country. He had not been married before and says he is leaving everything to me. What worries me is whether this means I must leave everything to him. Although I love him dearly, if I were to die first, he would have his cottage and enough to live on. I would like to leave the bulk of my estate to my children. I can't see it happening but I know that inheritances can set people at each other's throats; so, if my husband did want to claim my estate, could he do so?

A: You're right about wills causing trouble among the apparently closest families but in your case there should be no problem. You can leave your worldly goods to whomsoever you please and any challenge to your wishes will only succeed if you have failed to provide reasonable provision for someone who could have expected support from you.

In your case, your husband, though helpfully paying all the bills, has had the benefit of living in your property and has been able to use his capital to buy the cottage. He would seemingly be reasonably provided for if your children had the benefit of your estate, and there would be little prospect of succeeding in any challenge to your will.

Q: In September next year my fiancé and I are to be married. We have decided to record the occasion on a video. We asked permission of the deaconess and she agreed, but informed us that the organist is likely to charge performing rights. Can he do this?

A: By recording your ceremony, which will include the performance of the organist, he is able to make a charge which relates not to his playing at your wedding but for granting you the right to replay his performance when you show the video on later occasions.

Q: I was widowed and remarried, but my second marriage has ended in divorce and my ex-husband is claiming a share of the property which had been bought by my first husband and left to me in his will. Unfortunately there was a small mortgage outstanding when I remarried and this was paid off by my ex-husband in a lump sum after the wedding. He did, however, insist that I sign a document acknowledging receipt of the payment as a loan to be repaid to him. The property, which is in my name alone, has leapt in value and he now claims an entitlement to at least half. Where do I stand? Our marriage was a disastrous mistake and lasted only four years.

A: It is as well to stress that the court does have complete discretion to deal with any property as it thinks fit following the breakdown of a marriage. However, in view of the length of your marriage and the facts regarding the purchase and title of the house, we believe it is unlikely that your ex-husband will achieve his dizzy expectations. It may be that because he insisted upon paying off the mortgage as a loan, the court will hold that he is only entitled to repayment of this money plus some interest, and this sum is likely to be far less than a percentage interest in your house. In the end, all factors will be taken into account regarding your respective needs, obligations and assets before the final award, if any, is made on his application.

Q: My father is in the process of getting a divorce from his wife (not my mother).

He was married to her for just under two years when she left him to live with another man. Whilst my father was away for a few days, she returned to his house and removed as many of the household possessions as she could and they now furnish her new home. She also removed some of my father's personal possessions, leaving him with virtually nothing. Surely she is not entitled to these items as my father owned most of them before he met her?

A: If your father is in the process of getting a divorce, there is a procedure under the Matrimonial Causes Act whereby he can obtain an injunction against his wife for the return of his property. We would advise him to seek this injunction without delay as clearly she is not entitled to his personal possessions and it may well be that she is not entitled to a substantial amount of the household possessions which she has also taken. In Scotland, he should pursue an action for delivery.

Q: My husband and I have been married for six years. He had two children from his first marriage and he and I lived together for a time while waiting for his divorce. Only a nominal maintenance order was made for the ex-wife but he paid maintenance for the children, and when the sum was decided upon, my income was taken into account. The ex-wife has had regular employment and lives with her boyfriend, who also earns good money (although his income was not looked at for maintenance of the children). Now we are planning our own family and I will stop working. Can we have either the maintenance for the children or the nominal 5 *pence* a year order in favour of the ex-wife stopped? We cannot support two families on one income.

A: You can always return to the court and present new financial circumstances which might allow for a variation to ease the burden upon the paying party. In respect of the children, maintenance will not be stopped but will be ordered at the maximum amount considered necessary for them and reasonable for your husband to pay, taking his reduced income into account. Your own income was taken into consideration to help assess how much your husband could afford to pay. Therefore when you stop working, this factor, together with the added responsibilities of a new child, should be put forward to argue a reduction. From what you have said there seems no reason for the court to continue the nominal 5 pence order for the ex-wife at all.

Q: When my husband and I separated, we put some of our possessions in storage. Unbeknown to me, my husband removed a carpet of mine which I had bought before our marriage and subsequently sold it. He now refuses to pay me the £400 that the carpet was approximately worth. Can I sue him for theft and how do I stand legally?

A: On the facts of your letter, you can indeed sue your husband for theft – which in a civil action has the technical name of 'conversion'. Your husband has 'converted' your property into cash and you are now able to claim against him for its value.

Q: I've just discovered that the man I married six years ago is a bigamist. He has a wife and two sons at the other end of the country. Apart from being distraught on my own account, I'm desperately worried about our five-year-old daughter. Does this mean she is illegitimate? And, if so, what would her position be if my 'husband' dies? Would she be entitled to a claim on his estate if he died intestate?

A: You haven't said whether you were the first 'wife' in time. If you were, then clearly you and your children have all the normal rights and benefits arising out of marriage. But if you went through a wedding ceremony when a wife was already in existence, then

MARRIAGE AND DIVORCE

your entire marriage was nonexistent from the start. However, you are not in the position of a live-in lover because although the law says you are not and have never been a wife, you are entitled to claim maintenance for yourself and your daughter as if your marriage were valid. As for your specific question of your daughter, she is treated in just the same way as any other child of her father. There is no longer any distinction between legitimate and illegitimate children for the purpose of inheritance.

Q: My boyfriend split up with his wife six months ago. He is Muslim and he has asked me to marry him under Islamic law in a mosque to purify our relationship. Would this be seen as bigamy under English law? He has not divorced his wife.

A: You can happily go and be 'purified' with impunity! Such a ceremony would not be recognised as a marriage under English law and thus no question of bigamy arises. The other side of this, however, is that you gain no rights under the law and could make no claim as a 'wife' if your Muslim 'marriage' ended. Remember that under Islamic law all your 'husband' has to do is pronounce 'I divorce you' three times and it's done!

Q: After I divorced my first husband, he agreed I should have a house for me and our two children. We arranged to buy a property, which is now the subject of argument. The house was bought in his name to ensure that a mortgage could be granted and he loaned me half the deposit monies. Until my new man came on the scene, he also paid the mortgage instalments, but that was instead of maintaining the children. My new man has taken over all the outgoings on the house but my ex-husband is now threatening to claim for his share of the value of the property and force a sale of the house. We are very worried by this.

A: It is hardly surprising that you are worried by these threats and you must take immediate steps to prevent him selling without your knowledge – a solicitor will be able to deal with this through the local land registry. From what you have said, it does not look as if your ex-husband would have any claim to the property – only to the return of his loan of part of the deposit money. Since the house was bought after divorce, then the law would look at what was intended at the time of the purchase to decide whose house it is. It seems that the house was intended for you, and you should now take steps to have it transferred from your ex-husband's name – a fairly complex procedure for which you would be well advised to seek help from a solicitor. By the way, you can also claim maintenance for the children if you wish.

In Scotland, the situation is again different and the advice of a solicitor is essential.

Q: I am planning marriage and my fiancé and I have purchased a property upon which we are paying a large mortgage. We were both previously divorced and I have my three children living with us. I receive no maintenance for them as my ex-husband is unemployed. My fiancé has been paying £20 a week maintenance for his daughter but we are now finding these payments hard to meet in view of our mortgage commitment. My fiancé's ex-wife is also planning marriage. Could we realistically have the maintenance payments reduced?

A: Theoretically, any maintenance payment can be varied by agreement or application to the court. If the ex-wife is unwilling to agree to a reduction, be warned that it is unlikely that the court would reduce the sum since the maintenance is specifically for the child. The ex-wife's change of circumstances would have little bearing on your fiancé's responsibilities towards his daughter.

Q: My mother, who is now 61, is unhappily married. My stepfather keeps her short of money, is anti-social and pays no attention to her or to the home which they jointly own. My mother has to work in order to keep herself but her health is beginning to suffer. She would like a divorce but is worried that because my stepfather is 73, she would get nothing from the house if she left him.

A: Since the house is jointly owned, your mother has a legal entitlement to half its value. The court has wide powers to deal with property upon the breakdown of marriage and the difference in ages will not necessarily cause the court to interfere with your mother's legal rights. It may be a factor to be taken into account but it will be one of many considerations when all the needs and assets of both parties are looked at.

Q: I bought my flat a year before I married six years ago. Because we spent most of our married life overseas, my husband and I lived there together for a total of only seven months. We separated eighteen months ago and he took almost all our joint possessions because he was 'letting me keep the flat'. The mortgage is in my name only and he paid just a few hundred pounds towards the outgoings on the flat in the time we were married. My husband is now making a claim on half of the flat on the grounds that it was the 'matrimonial home'. I'm worried because I have heard that a man is entitled to two-thirds of all joint possessions when a couple without children splits up. When my husband left, he had more than £15,000 of his own in his bank account from the sale of the house that he owned before we were married. Can he really be awarded half the value of my flat?

A: The court has absolute discretion to make orders dividing up property between husband and wife as it thinks fit. There is no set formula to decide who gets what, so you can forget what you have heard. This old two-thirds/one-third rule was created by the courts as nothing more than a rough and ready guideline in a limited number of cases. From what you have told us, it would seem most unlikely that your husband would be entitled to any share in your flat. Indeed, he could find himself at the wrong end of your claim against the joint possessions that he helped himself to, particularly if you live in Scotland, where there is a presumption that you are entitled to an equal share of these when they are looked at with any other assets he has. You must seek expert legal advice, come what may.

Q: What is a legal marital relationship? I'm not talking about kinky sex! It's just that my husband died two years ago and I realise that I've fallen in love with his unmarried brother. I have two children from my marriage. My brother-in-law and I would love to get married.

A: In the sixteenth century Henry VIII tried, in vain, to have his marriage to Catherine of Aragon annulled on the grounds that the Church of Rome should not have sanctioned a marriage between a man and his brother's widow. He failed because Catherine's first marriage to Henry's older brother had never been consummated and had not therefore been a valid marriage.

Nowadays the civil law looks more tolerantly at marriage, but even so there are prohibitions on certain marriages between classes of relationships.

Most obviously, there cannot be a marriage

between siblings (brother and sister) or between 'lineal' relatives whether by blood or adoption (grandparent, parent or child) or even between uncles and nieces or aunts and nephews.

Some further restrictions govern marriages between the children of former spouses and the new husband or wife but you can see that your relationship with your brother-in-law is not within any of these prohibitions or restrictions. You can marry lawfully and we wish you happiness.

Q: I'm sixteen and my boyfriend is seventeen and we're very much in love. We want to get married but our parents won't give their permission. So what we want to know is if we can get married at Gretna Green? If we can, what are the rules: how long do we have to be in residence and could our parents stop the wedding? Also, would the marriage be valid in England?

A: Well, our immediate reaction is that you should wait and get married with both your families giving their blessings. Parents do know a thing or two about marriage, you know. However, if you are determined to go through with it, this is the situation:

As you are both minors, that is, under eighteen, your parents' consent is required to marry in England and Wales. As you are both over sixteen you do not require consent to marry in Scotland (Gretna Green being the first stopping post in Scotland over the English border). However, only in cases of exceptional urgency will a sheriff's licence be issued to dispense with the usual requirement of the proclamation of banns. Otherwise you have to make a joint application for the licence and at least one of you must have lived in Scotland for fifteen days before the application is made.

If you do go ahead with your marriage at Gretna Green, it will be valid and recognised in England –

but we stress you should think long and hard before taking such a serious step.

Q: My fiancé, who is Scottish, has paid maintenance voluntarily to his ex-wife, who still lives in Scotland. There are no dependent children and she is free and able to work. He also gave her the contents of their council house and three thousand pounds. He agreed to pay her the maintenance – called aliment – which he could afford at the time. Now he is frequently unemployed and finding it increasingly hard to meet these payments. I have advised him to stop paying as there was no court order – am I right?

A: Without a court order there is no enforceable agreement and your fiancé can either stop or reduce these payments at any time. However, such an action would be likely to prompt the ex-wife into an application to the court, which would then determine the level of maintenance to be paid, if any, upon hearing of the needs and assets of both your fiancé and his ex-wife. Your fiancé's ex-wife could apply to the court in Scotland to decide the question of maintenance and any judgment obtained by her can be both registered and enforced by the English court.

4. LIVE-IN LOVERS

Men and women are different – and that can lead to differences. And while love and marriage might not always go together, a live-in lover can be even more tricky. It's all right while the relationship is good but when it starts going wrong . . .

Q: I left my rented flat to move in with my boyfriend six years ago. He is buying his flat on a mortgage. It is in his name and he pays it, but we go halves on all the bills and I reckon I buy most of our food and drink. This didn't matter except we've been quarrelling a lot and are now splitting up. The trouble is that I've not enough to pay a deposit on a place of my own and the cost of rented accommodation has soared beyond my means. My ex-lover says it's not his problem and will give me nothing although we bought some of the furniture jointly. What is my legal position?

A: Apart from the furniture which you bought together and therefore own jointly, we regret that you have secured no property rights for yourself by paying bills or household expenses. The court has no power to make transfer of property orders in a case of cohabitation (unlike with a married couple) and you can, therefore, expect nothing unless you have legal title to it.

Q: My boyfriend and I bought a house jointly eight years ago. It was a bargain as it was in a terrible state, and we've since done it up. The neighbourhood has also gone up in the world so it's now worth a lot more. The problem is I've now fallen for someone else and he wants to marry me, and I like the idea suddenly. I want us to sell the house and go halves on the money but my boyfriend flatly refuses. He says he wants to stay in the house and will give me half of what we originally paid for it. This is obviously ridiculous. Can he do this?

A: No, he cannot! You are entitled to half its market value. In your case, you can make an application to the court for a declaration as to your half-share *and* an order for the sale of the house.

Q: My common-law husband was killed in a car accident last year when a lorry ran into the side of him. The lorry driver was at fault since he came out of a side turning without looking. I had been living with my common-law husband for four years and we had one child who is now three years old. As we were not legally married, am I able to make any claim for myself or our child?

A: Although not legally the widow, you are entitled to claim for yourself as if you were the widow because you had been living together for more than two years prior to the death of your cohabitee. Your claim will be on the basis of your dependency on his income, and the size of the claim will depend upon his earnings, prospects and age. You would not, unfortunately, be entitled to the modest sum for bereavement as this is payable only to spouses or mothers of under-age children.

Your child is entitled to be treated in exactly the same way as a legitimate offspring in any compensation claim.

In Scotland, you would have the rights of a widow by obtaining a court order confirming that you were 'married' by 'habit and repute'.

Q: I finished with my boyfriend six months ago and, since then, he's harassed me constantly. I get phone calls at all hours, often in the middle of the night. Or the phone rings in my office and the receiver is replaced when my colleagues or I answer it. I know it's him, really. And I've been receiving junk mail by the ton and I know he's behind it. I had a word with the police and they were very sympathetic but say there's nothing they can do unless I am physically harassed. Do you have any suggestions?

A: The police, rightly, will not intervene unless the criminal law is broken and, as they have told you, unless you are physically harassed. However, the civil law will come to your rescue, albeit on a carthorse rather than a charger. You will be able to apply for a court order against your ex-boyfriend to stop this harassment. This carries the threat of imprisonment for contempt of court if he does not obey the court order. The procedure, although effective, is somewhat cumbersome and you will probably need expert legal assistance to set it up.

Remember, too, that you must be absolutely certain – and able to persuade a court that it is your 'ex' who is causing all this trouble.

Q: Before I split up with my boyfriend we went on a two-week holiday in Tenerife. As he was unemployed at the time but about to start a new job, I agreed to lend him the money to pay his share of the holiday expenses, which amounted to around £250. Obviously I now want the money back, but he refuses to pay it in a lump sum, insisting he pay it at £10 a month because, he says, he is hard up. I know that he is earning more than I am now and don't see why he should get away with this. What do you suggest?

A: Well, you could take action against him and obtain a county or sheriff's court judgment for the full amount. Be warned, however, he will probably plead hardship to the court, who could very well be persuaded to permit him to pay you off at £10 per month – so you would be back to square one.

Q: My boyfriend and I are in the process of buying a house, but one thing is bothering me. If my boyfriend dies, who will get his share of the house? My boyfriend says I will, but I think it will be his next of kin, i.e. his mother. And there's no way I would want to share my house with her! I certainly hope nothing happens to either of us for a few years yet, but can you put my mind at rest?

A: It is very sensible to sort this out now. When you buy your house, make sure that it is purchased as a joint tenancy with a right of survivorship. This ensures that the whole property passes to whichever of you survives the other. That way, his mother won't even get a foot in the door! We do stress that you must make sure you tell your solicitor what you want at the time of the purchase, since this intention as to title has to be clearly stated on the transfer document.

Q: My boyfriend wants me to give up my council flat and move into his house with a view to marriage. I am uncertain as to whether I want to marry him but I am tempted to move in as he is willing to put his house into our joint names 'as a sign of good faith'. If I do move in but then do not marry him, will I be entitled to claim a share in the house if we separate in the future?

A: Not necessarily, is the short answer. It all depends upon the intention behind the transfer of the property. If it is your boyfriend's intention to make a gift to you of a share in his property, you would probably be able to establish a claim. If, however, the transfer was with a view only to marriage, then you might end up with nothing. It is essential, then, that the exact basis of your moving in and any transfer made is clearly spelled out – preferably with the advice and assistance of a solicitor *and* before you give up the security of your council house.

Q: My brother has lived with his girlfriend for ten years and they have just had a little girl. Does he have to adopt his own daughter in order to establish he's her father, or does he have the same rights as any married father?

A: Your brother has the rights of a married father only if he becomes one – although, for the most part, he has the obligations. When couples remain unmarried, all custody rights remain with the mother; and the father of an illegitimate child (now described as a 'non-marital' child) has no automatic rights even to access. He has the right (and sometimes the heartache), of applying for it if the mother is uncooperative. The differences are perhaps slight but they can be significant.

Q: I'm the single mother of a three-year-old boy. At the time he was conceived, I was living with a boyfriend. I was beginning to tire of the relationship and had had a couple of one-night stands. To be honest, I don't really know who the father is but my old boyfriend thinks it's him. I didn't want to marry him and I was given a council flat. I was also awarded £10 a week from my boyfriend who stated he was the father. I didn't want him to have access to my son and the court upheld this. Now he's sent a message via a friend to say he's getting fed up and is going to apply for a blood test to be taken to determine paternity. I'm so afraid. Can he insist on this, and if it's found he's not the father, will I have to pay back the money I've had from him to date?

A: Since it appears a court awarded you maintenance for your child, it is likely that your ex-boyfriend was adjudged to be the father. If he wanted to challenge this finding he would normally have 21 days in which to do it, but the court which hears the appeal from the order can extend the period – and can order blood tests if they consider that there are proper grounds for doing so. You don't have to cooperate with any blood-test order, but if you take that line the court can draw conclusions against you. If your ex-boyfriend's appeal were made within the 21-day period and successful, you could be ordered to repay monies received. If he appeals successfully at a much later date, the court would be unlikely to order you to repay the money unless you could easily afford to do so or if it was found that the original order was made as a consequence of deliberate deception on your part.

5. CHILDREN AND ANIMALS

As the saying goes: children are certain sorrow, uncertain joy. They may be a blessing but, sometimes, the blessing is heavily disguised.

We're not being facetious including animals in this chapter. They might not cause as many problems as children, but animal crackers is a very telling phrase!

Q: My second husband and I have been married for eight years. We have two lovely children, and my ten-year-old daughter from my first marriage lives with us. We're all so happy together that I'd like Susie to take my husband's surname so we can all feel like one family. Is this possible?

A: It is possible, but only if Susie's father is agreeable or the court sanctions the change. There usually has to be an exceptional reason to permit a child to be known by another name. An almost complete assimilation into a new family structure might suffice, as appears to be your case.

Q: I was adopted by my grandparents on my mother's side when I was three years old, following the divorce of my parents. I found out that my real father is a very wealthy man but I have had no contact with him since my adoption. I also discovered that my father remarried but had no other children. I now have an adult son of my own and I want to know whether I or my son could have any claim on my father's estate and if necessary could contest any will that he may make.

A: Once a legal adoption has taken place, the adopted child is treated in law as the child of the adopters and no-one else. Thus it seems that neither you nor your son has any legal claim on your father's estate or right to contest his will.

If, however, you wish to contact your father for personal reasons – or if an adopted person, on reaching eighteen, wishes to make contact with their real parents but has no knowledge of the parents' whereabouts or even identity – a call to the British Agencies for Adoption and Fostering on 01–407–8800, or in Scotland on 031–225–9285, or to the Salvation Army, will put you on the right track.

Q: My fiancé is divorced and his ex-wife has custody of their small daughter, who recently started school. He has discovered that the child has been enrolled at the school in her mother's maiden name. Although he has complained, the school refuses to do anything about it. He is really upset and wants to know if he can achieve anything by going to court about this.

A: Your fiancé's ex-wife is not entitled to change the surname of their child without good reason or his consent. Without delay, your fiancé can seek a court order against his ex-wife to ensure that his daughter is known both at school and generally by the name on her birth certificate.

CHILDREN AND ANIMALS

Q: When he was a child, my son had an illness which the doctors said could make him sterile. When his girlfriend told him she was pregnant and the child was his, he accepted this and married her. This marriage ended in divorce and he has met another girl he wants to marry. My question is whether he will still be liable to pay maintenance for the child of the first marriage if he now finds out he cannot have children after all?

A: When your son married and the child was born, your son, believing his girlfriend, undoubtedly treated the child as his own. He thus became legally liable for the child whether in fact he was the father or not. Even if he were to discover now that he is, and has always been, unable to have children, he could not walk away from his maintenance obligations to what the law describes as a 'child of the family'.

Q: My son attends a school where rugby is compulsory. I read recently that there are several thousand accidents on school sports fields each year, some of them very serious. It set me thinking what the legal situation is if a child is injured while playing sports at school. Who is responsible and is it possible to claim compensation?

A: Accidents at school are indeed more frequent than one might suppose, but generally a school authority is not insured for all accidental injury. If negligence or incompetence result in injury in the school playground, science lab or on the rugby field, then the school will be responsible and its insurers will probably pick up the appropriate tab.

Otherwise, you should check with the school as to whether there happens to be accident insurance in force. If not, and if you are worried, you should consider taking out a policy yourself.

Q: I am a nineteen-year-old student and I'm two months pregnant. I cannot possibly have the child. I've two more years of studies ahead of me and then I want to work before settling down. Also, although it sounds despicable, I realise I am not very keen on the father. I told him I was going to have an abortion. To my horror, he went completely wild, said he loved me deeply and wanted me to be the mother of his child. He says that he will take me to court to stop me terminating my pregnancy. Can he really do this? I'm going to have the operation anyway, but I'm worried in case he can take proceedings against me afterwards as he keeps going on about it being his child as well as mine. I'm desperately worried as I don't want either the college authorities or my parents to find out and he says he's going to make a 'stink' about it. I wish I'd never told him now but just gone ahead and done it.

A: However deeply he feels, the father of your unborn child cannot stop the termination of your pregnancy nor has he any grounds for 'proceedings' either before or after an abortion. Maybe the day will come when the wishes of the 'father' are taken into account in such circumstances – but we're not there yet. There is little you can do to stop him carrying out the threat to make public your predicament. But we're sure your parents and the college will show greater tolerance and sympathy. In the end we feel a woman must decide the best course for herself but must do it in a responsible way. It isn't very responsible to sleep with, let alone get pregnant by, a man you're 'not very keen on'.

Q: Do I have the right to see my grandchildren? I have fallen out with my daughter-in-law and she is trying to stop me seeing the children but I am prepared to go to court if necessary to maintain contact with them. Would the court help me?

A: The court will only consider an application by you if there already exists a court order regarding the legal custody of your grandchildren (following a divorce, for example) or where one of the children's parents (or both) are deceased. Another but remote possibility would be for you to attempt to have the children made wards of court and then apply for access, but your chances of success are slight and you would be unlikely to get legal aid. Difficult for you though it is, your best solution is to swallow hard and try to make it up with your daughter-in-law – for your sake and the children's.

Q: My boyfriend's ex-fiancée is pregnant and although he has her on tape saying that the baby is not his, he is quite sure it is. She told him she doesn't want him to see the baby when it's born and he says that this being the case he will not have to pay maintenance. Is this true? If she does want maintenance, would the tape stand up in court? If he does have to pay maintenance, will the court take into account hire purchase agreements he may have when they make their decision on how much he will have to pay? Also, if she decides not to claim maintenance now but changes her mind when the baby is older, can she still claim it?

A: You certainly have a lot of questions! Does your boyfriend ever get a word in edgeways?
 Even if your boyfriend does not see the child, it does not mean that he might not be ordered to pay maintenance if the court rules that the child is his. However, the mother would have to apply within three years of the birth and the tape would certainly be allowed in court, although it would not be conclusive. Your boyfriend's financial obligations would then be fully considered. However, the mother can apply at any future date if your boyfriend were to provide money or gifts for the child up to its third birthday,

thus implying he accepts paternity and, therefore, responsibility.

Q: I have traced my father after thirty years. I am his illegitimate daughter and my mother registered me as the daughter of the man she married before I was born. My father has a daughter by his marriage prior to my birth. Although I have no proof except my mother's word, my real father does accept me as his daughter. What I would like to know is, if my father were to die leaving no will, could I make any claim on his estate?

A: You most certainly can! Since 1969, an illegitimate child has had the same rights on the intestacy of a parent as if he were legitimate. Indeed, even if your father were to leave a will in which he referred only to his 'children', you would be included in that reference. If, as you say, your father accepts and looks upon you as his daughter then you might even be entitled to reasonable provision from his estate notwithstanding a will from which you were excluded – but that would be dependent upon the exact nature of your ongoing relationship and your needs, if any, at the time of his death. However, in the event of conflict over the estate, you must be able to satisfy a court that you are indeed your father's daughter.

Q: Five years ago, I had an affair with a man and had his child. I registered him in my name. Now the father has come back into my life and we want to be together. For financial reasons, I do not want to marry him but we are going to spend the rest of our lives together. We want Sam to have my lover's surname now. Can we change it on the birth certificate?

A: Once a birth certificate is completed it is virtually impossible to alter any details on it. Therefore your surname will remain on his certificate, but you can

CHILDREN AND ANIMALS

change his name by deed poll if you so wish. This, of course, applies to anyone wishing to change their name for whatever reason.

Q: My little daughter, aged six, was hit in the face by a stone during playtime at her school. Some children, it seems, were playing nearby and throwing sticks and stones but no teacher was there to supervise. She was lucky not to lose her eye but it looks as if she may have a permanent scar on her face. I am very upset about this. Is there anything I can do?

A: What an unfortunate occurrence! If there was no supervision at all then you could show inadequate care was being taken by the school. If, however, supervisors were about but just happened to miss a one-off throw, then it will not be quite so easy to show that there was lack of reasonable supervision. After all, the school can't provide watchers for each child all of the time. Since it rather suggests that this had been going on for a while, it ought, if a careful watch was being kept, to have been stopped. In short, depending on the facts, you may well have a good case against the school authorities for claiming compensation on behalf of your daughter.

Q: My dog is a normally well-behaved animal and I occasionally let him walk freely along our street. The other day, however, he ran into the road, causing a car to swerve. It missed the dog but hit a lamppost. Fortunately, no one was hurt, but am I liable for the car damage?

A: Both pets and young children should be firmly held at all times! As your dog was unrestrained then, yes, you could well be held responsible for the damage caused whilst the dog was under – or in this case, out of – your control. If you have no separate insurance for your pet, then check your household

insurance policy which ought to cover you for an event like this.

Q: My son lives at home and drives me mad. He does not pay for his keep. He stays up all night, leaving heaters on and lights on. He makes a mess of the house and he is unpleasant and uses foul language to both my husband and myself. He says he doesn't care for any of us and his moodiness and unpleasantness are causing distress to both my husband and myself. He is now 28. Is there any way we can get him to leave?

A: **Your son has only a licence to occupy your house and whichever of you or your husband owns the house can simply withdraw this licence. However, we strongly urge you to do this in writing and by means of a solicitor's letter, which will be sufficient to bring your son's occupancy to an end and hopefully give you and your husband the peace and tranquillity that you clearly desire – but prepare yourself for possible ugly scenes once you take this action.**

Q: My husband cannot take time off during the school holidays. We would like to take our children away during term-time but wonder what the position is. They are at a rather strict school and I'm slightly in awe of the headmistress myself so would like to have the facts at my fingertips.

A: **We're glad to hear there are some schools which care about education! In fact, you are quite within your rights to take your children away on holiday with you. But the regulations stress that, save in exceptional circumstances, only two weeks should be allowed in any one school year.**

Q: My son and his wife have separated and she has subsequently suffered a nervous breakdown. The social workers in charge of the 'case' are talking about our grandchild being taken into care. My husband and I adore the child and would love to have her live with us. Would it be possible for us to put this forward in court?

A: Why wait till it reaches that stage? Why not contact the social worker in charge and explain how much you would like to take the child and state your case for having her live with you. To answer your question, though, new rules were brought in in August 1988 to allow magistrates to rule that grandparents may be parties to care proceedings. But even if you are not, the court has power to award you care and control if it is considered to be in the best interests of your grandchild.

Q: Our fifteen-year-old son has made an eighteen-year-old girl pregnant. She led him on, but I can't deny he is very mature for his age. He is a very good student and we want him to have a good career and life. But the girl says she wants him to marry her when he is sixteen (in five months' time). She makes veiled threats of what she will do if he doesn't agree. We're worried sick. What is his legal position? Could he be taken into care? And what about financial responsibility? We cannot support another child and our son has years ahead of him before he gets a job. He doesn't want to get married but accepts that he is the father. Is there any way of establishing this for certain?

A: Your very 'mature' son was unfortunate indeed to get mixed up with a not very mature eighteen-year-old. Clearly any marriage between these two would be a recipe for disaster and your son should not be intimidated by threats to take a course which is undesired by him and undesirable for him. As to the legal position: no question of care arises unless your son is known to the authorities to be out of control and this incident is but one example of his general conduct. This seems hardly the case here. As to financial responsibilities! Well, if a child is born, he is the father and he is as responsible as the mother. An order for maintenance cannot be made against you as grandparents, but can be made against him when he reaches sixteen years old. As to the amount – this will be determined according to his income. If this is NIL – well, you cannot get blood out of a stone! And, after all, the lady in question can hardly have been unaware of her lover's position in the wide world. Your son admits that he is the father but if he wishes to challenge paternity when the child is born a test will be ordered. At the end of the day your son has got himself into a pickle and it is to be hoped that the innocent child produced doesn't suffer the most.

Q: My dog, who is very boisterous, jumped up at a friend to greet him and accidentally tore the sleeve off his jacket. My friend insists that I should buy him a new jacket but, to be honest, although it did come from an expensive shop, it wasn't all that new. I'll replace it for the sake of peace and harmony, but would like him to know that I'm not legally obliged to do so. Is that right?

A: Although your friend does have to buy a replacement jacket at today's prices, he seems prepared to make an unwarranted profit out of your good nature and your dog's exuberance.

You could argue, at a stretch, that you have no legal obligation to buy a replacement jacket if your friend was aware that you had such an enthusiastic pet prone to effusive greetings. More likely, you would be liable – but only to the extent of the value of the jacket just before it was torn.

You might well count your blessings that your dog did not knock your friend off his feet and cause more serious damage – to his person. Remember, people who own dogs must exercise control over them – or risk unleashing ill feelings in others!

Q: There is a local cat which frequents my back yard and my next-door neighbour's as well. The cat does nothing to provoke anyone, but even when it is in my back yard the neighbour throws stones at it. I have objected without success. What can I do?

A: The poor animal must be a masochist!
There is something you can do – certainly about your neighbour's charming pastime of aiming missiles into your yard. Your protests about the cat may get you nowhere but if you firmly point out to your neighbour that to throw anything, including stones, on to your property is actionable trespass and can and will be prevented by a county or sheriff's court injunction, then the cat and you should be spared any further trouble. If the cat has the sense that these animals are credited with, it will give your neighbour's property a very wide berth.

Q: A year ago our small daughter was viciously attacked by a Doberman Pinscher who ran into our garden. The dog was finally restrained and put down but my daughter was left with scarring on her leg. She is terrified of all dogs and is unsettled generally. We have never traced the owners but wish to know if there is any way we can claim compensation for her.

A: If there was some way of finding out who owned this animal then you could well have a claim for the terrifying assault suffered by your daughter. Regrettably, without this information neither you nor she seems to have any redress as this attack does not come within the ambit of a criminal injury.

Q: Please settle an argument. I say that religious instruction classes in school are compulsory. My friend says it's a matter of parental choice. Who is right?

A: Religion, sadly, can cause many arguments! However, in general parents have the right to have their children excluded from either religious assembly or instruction. In those schools which have a religious foundation, parents normally find that separate arrangements can be made for their children to opt out of religious activity altogether. In any state school, the parents are entitled to arrange for children to receive alternative religious instruction either in the school itself or outside, in school hours, as long as this does not interfere with their general schooling or with the school's programme.

Q: I have every reason to believe that my daughter has been put into a class which undermines her academic capabilities. She attends a multiracial school and many of her classmates have little command of English. The teachers spend a lot of time with them and my daughter is just not fully stretched. I've spoken to the headmistress but she talks about our all having to live in a multicultural society and implies I'm racist. I'm not. My daughter's classmates are delightful but she isn't able to communicate with them and she's the one who is going to suffer.

A: Of course you're not racist and it seems most unhelpful of the headmistress to resort to this argument when you have raised a legitimate problem and are genuinely concerned. The simple fact, however, is that if the school attended by your daughter is organised into classes of mixed ability (irrespective of race, colour or background), then there seems little you can do as long as your child remains at this school. If, however, the school does stream children according to their ability and attainment and you consider your daughter could be moved to a class more suited to her potential, then your first line of approach must be to her teachers. You can try to persuade the headmistress, through them, that your daughter is in the wrong class.

As a last resort you could make enquiries of other schools in your local catchment area and if one suits, you should approach your local education authority and see if a place could be found for your daughter at another school. This is difficult to accomplish but at least worth a try! Finally, if the local education authority can be shown to be failing to provide a place for your child appropriate to her age and ability, then the Secretary of State for Education can intervene.

6. OTHER PEOPLE'S BABIES

Artificial insemination. Private adoptions. Surrogate motherhood. This is a whole new area for lawyers and definite guidelines are now being drawn up. However, women are worried about their legal position *now* since this 'brave new world' is already with us.

Q: I have agreed to be a surrogate mother for a couple I know for £2,000. Is this legal?

A: Surrogacy, which is a pregnancy and birth by one woman on behalf of another with the express intention of handing over the child at birth, seems for many childless couples the answer to their prayers.

The subject of surrogate motherhood is at present governed by the Surrogacy Arrangements Act 1985, which makes it unlawful to arrange a surrogate pregnancy for gain. The unlawfulness does not extend to the pregnant woman or to the childless parents. You may be acting legally, therefore, but you should know that neither you nor the hopeful parents can enforce any such agreement between you in the courts. You cannot successfully sue for payment; they cannot force you to hand over the child.

There is also some doubt as to the lawfulness of payment to a private clinic which may have participated in the surrogate pregnancy by the process of artificial insemination – although, curiously, such a pregnancy would appear to be acceptable if it could be achieved under the National Health.

Finally, a child born to a surrogate mother cannot legally be handed to the childless parents without the intervention and approval of an official adoption agency.

Q: My husband and I are unable to have children of our own and we have been turned down for adoption because of our ages (we are in our late thirties), and because we follow different religions (this has never caused any friction between us; I think I may say we are very tolerant people). Recently, I got to know a young, unmarried mother of an adorable two-year-old daughter. She would like to go to London to make a fresh start and we would love to adopt the child. Is this possible to arrange? The girl is willing but are there any snags to a private adoption, like the mother claiming her back sometime in the future?

A: You are not, unfortunately, able to arrange a private adoption and have it sanctioned by the court in these circumstances. All adoptions of children in the United Kingdom have to be approved through a recognised adoption agency. Your only hope might be to have the mother give you actual custody of her child; if the child lives with you as effective foster parents for at least five years, you might then be able to go through with an adoption. Of course the risks of this are obviously that the mother could reclaim her child and you are by no means guaranteed an adoption at the end of the five years.

Q: My sister sadly can't have children. A year ago she unwisely agreed to a friend of hers having a baby for her. She was promised a lump sum when the baby was born and lived with them for the last three months of her pregnancy. Now what I always feared has happened; the baby has been born but my sister's friend won't give it up. She claims that as no legal contract was ever signed and no money was exchanged my sister has no rights over the child, even though my brother-in-law is the father. What can my sister do?

A: Unhappily, your sister can do nothing at all. She has no legal right to this child and your brother-in-law has only limited right to apply for access or custody, as would any father of an illegitimate child.

Q: After extensive testing, my husband and I have been told that we will not be able to have a child. The problem lies with me and I am depressed beyond words. Now a friend has agreed to enter into a surrogacy arrangement – she will (hopefully) become pregnant by my husband. Assuming all goes well, where do we stand as parents when the baby is born and handed over to us?

A: You have to adopt the child formally before you will be its parents legally and you and your husband have to be acceptable to the adoption agencies and social services even though your husband is the 'natural' father. Therefore you could find yourselves heartbroken at the end of the day if the authorities refuse to sanction the adoption. However, if the baby is with you soon after birth and you are obviously loving, caring and able to provide a suitable home, it is likely (but not certain) that you will be able to go ahead with the adoption.

Q: We've longed for a child for many years without success. We've been turned down for adoption on the grounds of age. Now, an American friend has told me that she can buy a baby for us in South America. I know the word 'buy' seems awful but we would love and cherish a child, believe me. I want our friend to go ahead but my husband is worried about legal implications. If we bring the child here, can we register him or her as our own? Would the baby be a British subject and entitled to a British passport eventually? Please advise us of any pitfalls which might arise.

A: One immediate problem would be if the baby had been obtained from a notorious 'baby farm' and its natural mother sought its return. No British court would recognise any contract to 'buy' a child as legal or binding, and we doubt you would have much chance to keep the child if the mother sought its return – nor would you get your money back.

However, if a legal and genuine adoption can be undertaken in the child's country of origin, then the practical arrangements are that the child receives authorised entry papers for admission to the UK, which are probably for some six months' duration initially but can be renewed. You must work with the Official Solicitor, or in Scotland, a curator appointed by the court, who represents the child's interests, and an independent social worker, who will liaise with the Official Solicitor (curator) and the courts. Eventually an adoption is arranged in this country, after which, of course, the child acquires British citizenship and is entitled to be treated in all ways as your natural child. Good luck!

7. MEDICAL MATTERS

It appears to be easier to take out an appendix than extract information from a medical man. To get hold of medical records or just get a straight answer, you often come up against a hospital screen. But we do have rights so it's worth persevering.

Q: I am going to change my doctor because I have not been very satisfied with her. I've just managed (with the help of my husband) to get off the tranquillisers she prescribed for me. I feel she might have implied in my medical records that I'm a nervous, slightly nutty, sort of person – I promise you I'm not, especially now – and I'd like to see what she has written about me. She refuses to let me see them. Can I insist? I don't want to get off on the wrong footing with my new GP.

A: The medical records remain the property of your doctor and you have no right to insist on seeing them. The records are not in themselves privileged – there's no such thing in Britain as medical privilege – but,

MEDICAL MATTERS

for all practical purposes, the only time you get to see these records is by obtaining a court order in connection with any legal proceedings in which they are relevant.

Q: Six years ago, my son went into hospital for a routine operation. Because of negligence, he came out severely brain-damaged. He requires constant attention as he now has the mental age of a six-year-old (he's eighteen). We sued the medical authorities and our solicitor advised us to accept the £5,000 offer of compensation. As you can imagine, the money has long since been swallowed up. At a local meeting of parents of disabled children last week, I met a woman who had undergone a similar experience. But she had been awarded £150,000. She told me I obviously had picked the wrong solicitor. But how do you get the right one for your case? And can I take any action against the man who advised me to settle for so little?

A: It is impossible to know who is or is not the right lawyer for the job, but some firms of solicitors specialise in different fields and medical negligence is one. It would have been worth finding a specialist firm by either making enquiries amongst the very group you belong to, or directly to the appropriate Law Society (see Appendix).

As to whether the compensation you received was adequate, this depends upon the facts of the case and if you could prove negligence. If you could, or if negligence were admitted, then you might well have a claim against your solicitor for wrong advice. The claim would be brought in the name of your son. Because he is now eighteen years old but with a young mental age, this would probably require the intervention of the Official Solicitor (curator in Scotland). In the first instance, find a specialist firm who will advise you on the chances of success – and on the more than usually complicated procedure for bringing a claim against your former solicitor.

Q: I'm a 26-year-old married woman and mother of two. A year ago, I had an affair with a man I'd met at the tennis club. It petered out, but I had a telephone call from him last month and he told me that he is HIV positive and his partner (a man – he also confessed to me that he is bisexual) is an AIDS patient. I told my husband that night as I love him very much and knew it wasn't fair to put him at risk (if I've not already done so). He was horrified, moved into the spare room and tells me he wants a divorce.

I will, of course, be going to my doctor and am praying that I don't have the virus but, if I do, do I have any comeback against this man who has literally ruined my life?

A: What a tragic outcome for you from this episode of casual philandering. Morally this man has a lot to answer for, but legally you have no more comeback on him than if you had caught flu.

Unhappily, the result of your affair is far reaching and teaches us all that the days of 'free love' may well be over as the consequences (as you have so painfully discovered) may far outweigh their transient pleasures.

We hope by now your tests have proved negative and you can start afresh.

Q: I am sixteen and earn a very low wage. I have been told that I need extensive dental work done but I am very worried about the cost and wonder whether I am entitled to have the treatment carried out on the National Health. I simply cannot afford to pay for it and neither can my parents.

A: As you are under eighteen, you are entitled to attend for your necessary dental treatment and receive it free of charge, irrespective of your income. However, we should emphasise to everyone that whether you are dealing with a dentist, builder or hairdresser, you should establish in advance what the cost will be.

Q: Last year I suffered a miscarriage during the early months of pregnancy, which caused me great distress. I now believe that this occurred because I was prescribed certain drugs by a locum doctor who was running my GP's practice whilst she was on holiday. I feel that I should be able to claim for all that I have gone through but my GP refuses to release my medical records, claiming that they are 'privileged'. Is there anything I can do?

A: Yes. Medical records are not 'privileged' – contrary to the popular belief. Although the British Medical Association has recently voted against the idea of doctors allowing patients to see their records, this does not affect your right to obtain an order through the courts compelling your doctor to produce your records, with a view to possible litigation.

Q: I had an operation two years ago to improve my nose. It was done privately and I discussed it fully with the surgeon in advance. When I was visited the following day, it was by a completely different man who said he was my surgeon's partner and had done the operation. I'm not very happy with the result of the operation and I'm furious that it wasn't performed by the man I discussed it with. Can medical people do this and do I have any comeback?

A: How very distressing for you. Whether the man was better or not than his partner, you have the right to the person you consulted and, more importantly, contracted with. Generally, private operations are governed by an agreement between the patient and the particular surgeon, and if the surgeon fails to carry out the operation, he is liable to you if something has gone wrong or if you have paid for services which you never received. As with any claim which involves injury to the person, you have three years in which to bring your case from the date that the injury occurred – in this case your operation.

Q: What sort of comeback does a person have in the case of wrong diagnosis. I had a smear test recently and was told everything was all right. But you do read of cases where women are diagnosed as 'negative' and then they develop cancer.

A: The theoretical answer is that any wrong diagnosis might be the result of a negligent act on the part of the person making it, and a claim can be made to cover the consequences of such a diagnosis – as it can be with any medical negligence.

In practical terms, however, it is very rare indeed to sue the medical profession successfully since it is so difficult to establish that they have acted unreasonably or negligently.

Q: Cervical smears and breast screening tests are recommended but they're not so easy to get. I had a smear two years ago and everything was supposed to be all right but now I'm not so sure and I'd like to go back for another. Do I have a right to insist upon another test now even though I am not strictly due for one for at least another year?

A: If you have genuine concerns and wish these to be investigated, then any reasonable doctor could be expected to act upon these and provide a suitable test for you.

If a doctor unreasonably fails to respond to your fears and you become ill as a consequence, then you would be entitled to make a claim against a doctor

and he could be liable to you for any pain and suffering you have – whatever small comfort that might be!!

Q: I cannot talk to my daughter about anything at the moment. She's fifteen and mixes with a crowd we know very little about. She doesn't appear to have a regular boyfriend but I think she is on the Pill. Don't the parents of under-age girls have the right to know if this is the case? Personally, I disapprove of the Pill strongly, not on moral but on medical grounds.

A: Your point of view was debated right up to the House of Lords, who finally decided that parents do not have the right to know if their doctor has prescribed the Pill for under-age daughters.

Perhaps if you do find you can't talk to your daughter, you might try writing to her as you have done to us. You could put down all your fears for her health and safety and show her how much you care.

Q: I'm one of those people who are too nervous to contradict a doctor, so now I've found a lump in my breast and I'm extremely worried. I'm determined to assert my rights (if any) and say that I don't want a mastectomy until all possible forms of alternative treatment have been discussed. But I'm told that I'll have to sign a form before the biopsy, agreeing to the removal of the breast if the biopsy is positive. What are my rights?

A: You should never be nervous about speaking your mind or voicing your concerns to anyone – and this includes members of the medical profession. Indeed, you do have the right to insist upon only the biopsy being performed without the removal of the breast should the biopsy prove positive. However, the surgeon can refuse to carry out the biopsy if he considers it inappropriate to be bound by only a limited consent. If he does refuse, you can ask either him or your own GP to refer you to another specialist who might be more sympathetic and willing to act upon your wishes. Before entering hospital it's best to find out what the surgeon's reaction will be to your views.

Q: I have been referred to hospital for a gynaecological problem. My own doctor is a woman and very sympathetic; she makes me feel relaxed and unembarrassed. But she says she doesn't know whether I'll see a man or woman at the hospital. Do I have any rights in this matter?

A: You have the right to make a request but, sorry, that's as far as it goes. We do understand your feelings. It's rotten being below par and then facing up to something or someone who adds embarrassment to your condition. All we can say to you is: please, put your health first and see the doctor as a doctor, not as a male or female. Most doctors or hospital authorities will do their best to act upon any request you make, but it just isn't possible to stipulate in these circumstances unless, of course, you can afford to go privately.

Q: I recently applied for life insurance and have been turned down. I wonder whether this has anything to do with the medical report from my doctor which the company asked for. I am in good health but I do have a stressful job and have seen my doctor occasionally when I have had difficulty sleeping. Is there some way I can find out why I was turned down and what was contained in this report?

A: Yes, under the new Access to Medical Reports Act of 1988, your doctor must show you a copy of his report unless he feels in his professional judgment that it would not be in your interest to see part or all of it. This must be done within six months.

If, for any reason, you had wanted to know what the doctor was going to write *before* the insurance company saw it, you should have contacted him within 21 days. Any insurance proposal form will include details for making these arrangements with your doctor.

We do feel that, for your own peace of mind and whether the doctor is willing to show you the report or not, you should go along to see him. After all, he might just tell you that it's not a good idea to smoke a hundred cigarettes a day!

8. MONEY MATTERS

As we know, it's not money but the love of lucre which is the root of all evil and this can lead to monumental rows. However, you don't have to be totally money-grabbing to affirm your rights in some cases. So, if you're someone who expects – quite rightly – her just desserts, we may have some answers for you.

Q: My aunt died recently aged 79. She had two sons and a daughter, none of whom visited her until her final illness. I lived nearby and popped in most days to see her. She had always complained about her children and said she was leaving everything to me. Over the years she gave me odd pieces of jewellery, including her beautiful diamond engagement ring. She died intestate, however, so I think the money will go to her children, who are already arguing among themselves. What upsets me is not the money but the fact that her older son says he wants the engagement ring back. He has virtually accused me of getting it from her while she was ill and says it was promised to him for his wife. It isn't true. What can I do? I'd like the ring as a memento because I loved the old lady dearly.

A: As your aunt gave you the ring while she was alive, you are entitled to keep it as it does not form part of her estate. If her greedy son contests your entitlement, he will have to prove that you exercised undue influence over his mother which led to her giving you the jewellery. Given the facts stated, it is doubtful that he would take action, let alone succeed.

Q: At work, I belong to a pools syndicate of six people and we all pay in a pound a week. There's one girl who is always forgetting to pay and she's even missed a few weeks so we've made up the difference. Last week, we won £30 and she hadn't paid but we still split it six ways. However, thinking ahead hopefully to a bigger prize, we wonder what her legal position would be if we'd made up her stake and then hit the jackpot. Would she be entitled to a sixth of the money?

A: If you agree between the five of you to include your sixth member as part of a syndicate then she could well be entitled to claim her share – less her stake money. If, however, you object to her taking advantage of your generosity, you should make it clear *now* that if she does not pay on time, she will be excluded from any money you win.

Q: My car was severely damaged when my husband, who was driving it, skidded on oil and drove into a wall. My insurers have so far refused to pay me out, on the basis that I did not name my husband as a likely driver when I filled out the proposal form and he had had a drink/driving conviction and a twelve months' ban about three years ago. I did pay a premium for comprehensive and 'any driver' insurance, so I cannot understand how they can be entitled to adopt the attitude they do. Can you advise me?

A: Most insurance companies ask the question and expect an answer as to who, apart from the insured, is likely to drive the car. A husband or wife is often an obvious candidate, and if they or anyone else is named, the insurance company expects to be told about their driving record since it might affect the amount of the premium and even whether cover will be granted at all. Your insurers are clearly suspicious that you omitted to name your husband on the proposal form precisely because of his drink/driving conviction. Ultimately, the facts regarding this omission will be the deciding factor as to whether you can persuade your insurers (or a court) that they ought to pay up for the damages under the terms of your policy.

Q: My father is eighty and lives alone. He's fiercely independent but he is becoming increasingly forgetful. Sometimes I find gas and electricity bills that are long overdue for payment. I'm afraid he might be cut off and have to pay to be reconnected, not to mention having to manage without these services in the interim. Is it possible for me to sign cheques on his behalf?

A: No. But your father can grant you a power of attorney or, in Scotland, a deed of factory and commission, which allows you to take over the management of his money when he cannot do it himself.

Where available you can use a special form called an 'Enduring Power of Attorney', obtainable from law stationers or from the Oyez Stationery Group, 159 Bermondsey Street, London SE1 4PU. The form isn't a very easy one so you might want the help of a solicitor in drawing it up.

Your father has to be fully aware of what he is doing when he grants you power of attorney, otherwise it will be invalid.

For information leaflets on enduring powers of

attorney, write to Public Trust Office, Protection Division, Stewart House, Kingsway, London WC2B 7JX.

Q: For the last twenty years, I shared a flat with my brother, who died six months ago. He had lived in the flat for ten years prior to my moving in. Although the tenancy was in his name, we split rent and all other expenses down the middle. Two months after his death, I had a letter from the owners of the property, saying they wanted vacant possession within two months. The company is registered in the Dutch West Indies. I consulted a solicitor and he told me that if I wanted to fight the case, counsel's opinion would have to be sought. I gave him £500 to cover costs.

I thought I would get the services of a barrister but didn't. We did get counsel's opinion but when we appeared in court, my solicitor did not speak at all. I was given an extra two months before eviction and now I've literally nowhere to go. The council has a waiting list for accommodation and can only offer me bed and breakfast. I hate the thought of this. I'd have to put my furniture in store and share a kitchen.

The flat I've lived in for so long is worth about £100,000 now as it's in a gentrified area. I couldn't begin to afford it and it seems unfair that we've paid a fair rent for thirty years and lived in the neighbourhood all our lives and now I'm being pushed out by a wealthy property company.

A: We couldn't agree more. It's totally unfair and insidious to see outsiders moving in and putting the genuine local people out of their homes. Unfortunately, all those years you have occupied the flat gave you no legal status. You were merely your friend's licencee, and whilst your friend as tenant could not have been evicted at the whim of the landlords, you have acquired no protection at all. Your landlords have already demonstrated their lack of concern for your predicament by taking possession proceedings against you and, although you haven't said so, it seems likely that the opinion from counsel rather confirmed your unhappy situation. What a shame that years ago you did not think to attempt to negotiate a joint tenancy with your friend. If this had been granted, it would have given you the same security of tenure as that enjoyed by your friend or close member of her family.

Q: I have almost completed the sale of my flat. How long will the solicitor hold the money?

A: Provided everything is in order, the Law Society says the money should reach you on completion. If it does not, you are due for interest on the money held.

If you have any cause for complaint, write to the Solicitors' Complaints Bureau, Portland House, Stag Place, London SW1E 5BL (or see Appendix).

Q: In my pay packet last week, I discovered that twice my usual wages had been put in although my pay slip was for the normal amount due. As this was clearly paid by mistake, I returned the extra to my employers – but would I have been entitled to keep it as I had received it innocently?

A: Your receipt of the extra money was innocent but once the mistake was discovered and you realised that you were not entitled to it then any retention of the money would have been theft and you were right to have returned it. We trust your employers fully appreciate your honesty and integrity.

Q: I am worried because my husband refuses to make a will. He says that I would get everything when he dies and I would have no problems. We have two young children and my husband has a child from a previous marriage? Is he right?

A: Where there is no will, the surviving spouse is now entitled to the first £75,000 of the deceased's estate. So your husband would be right if, on his death, he left assets not exceeding that amount. Once the estate goes above this amount, all the children, including those of a former marriage, are entitled to their half-share of the remaining portion of the estate. You would not, therefore, inherit everything if your husband is likely to leave assets in excess of £75,000 in England. The rules of intestacy differ slightly in Scotland.

Q: I have been living with my boyfriend for just over three years now. We are buying a house and it is in joint names. Six months ago his mother and father asked me to be a witness to their will – which I agreed to. Now I am worried that my boyfriend will lose his legacy and everything will go to his two brothers – one of whom is left only a small sum of money; the rest of his parents' belongings are to be split between my boyfriend and the other brother. We also intend to marry within the next two years.

A: Your concern is understandable but do be reassured that your relationship with your boyfriend will not affect his entitlement under his parents' will and neither will your marriage to him at a later stage. It has been settled law for more than a hundred years that where a will has been executed, the subsequent marriage between a beneficiary and a witness to the will does not affect the provisions of the will.

Q: Last year I was offered the chance to buy my flat for a good price as a sitting tenant. I have taken six months to make up my mind to buy and in that time the landlord has upped the price by £7,000. I am prepared to pay this but on condition he renovates my garage, which is in a somewhat sorry state. He is refusing to do this. How do I stand, legally, on this matter.

A: As a sitting tenant you cannot insist on the right to purchase the flat and it is up to your landlord whether he wants to sell to you and at what price. You are not, therefore, in a position to set conditions on the purchase – you can only negotiate and hope to find agreement by way of compromise. If it is still a good price, you ought to make up your mind before another six months elapse and the price goes up again.

Q: Are we responsible for our son's debts? He is an eighteen-year-old student and has overdrawn heavily at the bank.

A: Some of those bank advertisements have a lot to answer for! Teenagers become seduced into getting themselves in over their heads and mums and dads are then called upon to bail them out. However, you have no legal obligation to discharge your son's debts. He is over the age of majority and responsible for himself. Unless you have agreed with the bank to be a guarantor of your son's overdraft debt, the bank cannot look to you, simply as a parent, to make good the money owed by their customer, your son.

Q: I hope this doesn't sound too mean but I am the youngest of three sisters. The eldest has had no contact with the family for years, choosing to ignore all of us including our father, who died a short while ago. Although our father made a will leaving everything to all three of us in equal shares, he did alter the will by crossing out my elder sister's name and initialling the alteration, intending only myself and my middle sister to benefit. We have been told that this alteration does not have legal effect and the will is to stand as originally drafted. Is this right? And does it make any difference that the will had been altered at the offices of my father's solicitor and apparently with his approval?

A: It is indeed right in England that such an alteration will have no legal effect. To alter a will as your father wished, there should have been a new document drawn, called a codicil, or better still a fresh will made. However, if the attempted alteration was made while your father was receiving the 'benefit' of legal advice from his solicitor, then the solicitor ought to have known better. He could well be liable to you and your middle sister for your losses under the will because your eldest sister is now taking the share that your father finally intended her not to have. In Scotland such an alteration may be effective if it is authenticated. You should put this matter into the hands of a *competent* solicitor.

Q: I bought a second-hand car through the evening paper and paid cash for it. I tested it myself and it seemed fine, and because the owner assured me that he had had no trouble with it I went ahead with the purchase. I've only had the car for a month and I've been told by my garage that the engine will need to be replaced at great cost. Can I return the car and get my money back?

A: Possibly, if you are able to prove that when you bought the car the condition of the engine was such that even the most ignorant of car owners *must* have known that the car would require major surgery and the statement that the owner had had no trouble must have been false. In practice, it is not always easy to prove and generally you are far less protected in any private sale than if, for example, you had bought from a dealer. This is why people are advised to use experts from the motoring organisations to check over cars before they go ahead and buy them in private deals.

Q: My father died two years ago and left our home jointly to my elderly mother and me. I am an only child and expect to inherit the remaining half of the property from my mother, together with the remainder of my parents' estate. However, my mother has befriended a young neighbour who is turning her against me and I now believe that this young woman may be influencing my mother to change her will in favour of herself and her children. Do I have any redress if I find that this is in fact the case?

A: If on her death you find that your mother had changed her will in favour of this neighbour, you might well be able to challenge it. First, the court would have to be satisfied that your mother was of sound mind when her last will was made. Then the serious issue of undue influence on the part of this young woman could be considered. Finally, you might be entitled to claim under the Inheritance (Provision for Family and Dependents) Act 1975 that you have not been given reasonable provision under your mother's will. You should seek the services of a solicitor should your worst fears be realised.

Q: In January I ordered some goods from a mail-order company whose order form I cut out from their small catalogue. The price I paid included an insurance charge of 20 pence but the goods have never arrived. Unfortunately, the order form contained the company address and of course I no longer have this and it appears nowhere else in the catalogue. How do I stand with the insurance?

A: Well, of course, if you trace the insurers then you would be able to trace the company and demand to know the whereabouts of your goods. It is difficult to advise on your insurance position without knowing the terms upon which cover was effected and, indeed, whether it was effected at all. You must try to trace the company by seeing if you can get hold of another catalogue, scouring the newspapers for further company offers or even, if the company is limited and you can recall its full name, you might consider it worthwhile contacting Companies House to request a company search which would reveal an address.

Q: My husband and I are pensioners and we have our home and all our savings in joint names. When we both die, we intend the whole of our estate to be divided equally between our two married children. Is there any advantage or purpose in our making wills as on the first death the remaining partner will automatically inherit the whole estate? Is it not enough to make a will when only one of us is left?

A: Generally, it is sensible for each of you to make a will but if all of your estate is jointly owned then the survivor will automatically inherit everything, and this is one situation where we agree that there seems no need for a will to be drawn up until one of you has passed away. We strongly recommend a will be made at that stage since it is always easier to deal with an estate under a will than under intestacy.

Consider though, however unlikely it might seem, that you might both die at the same time – in a car crash, for instance. It would be terrible if the grief of your children were compounded by problems with inheritance.

Q: Can you please tell me who will benefit from an estate where the deceased was a bachelor and whose only surviving family are two brothers and two sisters? Is the estate shared equally or does it all go to the eldest brother or sister?

A: In the case of an intestacy where there are only surviving brothers or sisters, the estate is divided equally between them with no distinction being made as to their seniority.

Q: My car broke down some miles from home. I pushed it off the main road, but after locking it I had to leave it as I had an important appointment. I was unable to organise a garage to collect the vehicle for some ten days but when I returned with the mechanic to the spot where I had left the car we discovered it had been completely vandalised. My insurance company are now reluctant to meet my claim, saying that I was negligent in abandoning the car and not dealing with it sooner. Can they really refuse to pay me out?

A: Generally, insurance covers negligence – whether your own or others. Your insurers would have to show that your conduct was so irresponsible as to amount to a reckless disregard for your vehicle before they could refuse to pay you out. Since you had to leave the car but returned to deal with it at the earliest opportunity available, it seems that you could insist on a settlement. However, you should seek legal advice to check your policy – which is all-important in deciding whether or not you acted in clear breach of any of its terms.

Q: I recently bought a car through an advert in the local paper, only to find that the car had been stolen and was sold to me with false number plates and false registration documents. The seller has now disappeared.

Do I have any rights to resist the original insurers of the car, who are now claiming that they own the car and are seeking its repossession?

A: Unfortunately for you and your hard-earned, now sadly departed cash, you acquired no right of ownership (title) when you purchased the car since the 'seller' had no such rights to pass on to you. The insurers, no doubt, paid out when the car was stolen and they, therefore, became the legal owners and are entitled to possession of the car. You, regretfully, became the innocent victim whose rights and money disappeared into the night with the rogue who sold you a financial disaster.

Q: I am a widow with two married daughters and three grandchildren, and I wish to make a will. I have a house and some money, but I want to divide it up so that the grandchildren will each have something – and also a niece and nephew of whom I am very fond. I really feel that what I want to do is simple enough not to need a solicitor. Do you think that I am being unwise and should I seek legal help?

A: If you feel that your wishes are quite straightforward and your estate fairly uncomplicated to sort out, then you ought to be able to make your own will. There are printed forms, obtainable from stationers such as OYEZ, which can guide you. Certain fundamental points have to be followed though and these are: the will must be in writing and stated to be your last will; you must make sure that all your property and money is disposed of in the will; you must clearly identify the persons benefiting from your will (the beneficiaries) and you should make sure that at least two persons (as you are leaving property) are named as executors to deal with the estate. The executors can be beneficiaries – unlike the witnesses (at least two), who must see you and each other sign the will on completion. Finally, if you want to change anything after the will is drafted, you cannot simply cross out and alter the writing. You must either draft a whole new document or draw up a small addition to the will – called a codicil – which must be signed and witnessed formally.

If you have any real doubts about whether you can draw up a will yourself, you are well advised to see a solicitor. It does rather defeat the point if you think you have saved expense by doing it yourself but then the whole estate is eaten up in legal fees to sort it out afterwards.

Q: My husband and I took out an insurance policy to cover the contents of our house. Following a burglary we now discover that we were 'underinsured', which means that we only get back from the insurers a proportion of our losses. We took advice from an insurance broker, who assured us that we were fully covered and even helped us fill in the proposal form. The insurance company refuses to budge, however, and now it seems that after the distress of our home being broken into, we can't even be fully compensated!

A: It's worth remembering that when you rely upon an insurance broker or agent, he normally acts on your behalf and not on behalf of the insurance company. Therefore, if you received wrong advice, as seems to be the case here, the insurance company is not liable. If, however, the broker is worth suing, you would probably have a remedy against him – and if your failure to receive full compensation was proved to be caused by following his 'advice', you should be able to make up your losses from him.

Q: I renewed my insurance cover for two rings a few months ago and I recently lost one of the rings. I have claimed from the insurance company but they have refused to pay me as they say I did not tell them that my husband had had a conviction for dishonesty in the past year! Surely what my husband does should not affect me? The policy was in my name and I have always paid it.

A: It is a tough decision and one perhaps worth pressing with the insurance company, but legally they are entitled to take advantage of any fact that might be regarded as 'material to the policy' and which has not been disclosed to them. Even if you cannot see the importance or relevance of certain facts, you are under an obligation to provide full and frank details of anything which might affect the insurance company's attitude. Otherwise they invariably have an 'out' in accordance with the small print of the policy. It is essential to read the policy document carefully and, if in any doubt, to provide the information or seek assistance from the insurance company itself.

Q: I have been married and divorced twice and for the past ten years have lived happily with my lover. He is divorced. Neither of us has any children but he has a sister and three nieces on whom he dotes. He tells me that in his will he has left me the house we live in (it's his and in his name). I'm perfectly happy to continue as we are as I've not exactly been an advertisement for happy marriage, but a friend of mine has been sowing seeds of doubt in my mind. I'm not a gold-digger and I don't want to be whatever you call an unmarried widow but I would like to feel that the house is definitely mine. I have no doubts that the house has been left to me, but could his family have any claims on it? They have, incidentally, been provided for in the will. The point my friend makes is that unmarried people just do not have the same rights as a spouse, however long and close the relationship and whatever the terms of a will. Is this so? I would like to know any snags in continuing as I am now.

A: We hope you won't be an 'unmarried widow' (we can't think of a good word for it, either) for many years to come. But we would stress the importance to you and to married people as well – which means everyone – of making a will and getting all arrangements sorted out. It's not a question of being a gold-digger. It's a matter of sensible planning, just as you'd plan a holiday or organise a mortgage or think about your job prospects. It is a fact that a widow might be in a stronger position to resist any claim by other members of the family who might seek to upset the terms of a will. However, the size of the estate, the relationship of all parties, including yourself, to the deceased, your means, the assets of the other relatives and their expectations are all matters which have to be considered in the event of any claim being made.

Q: I left my car for an hour and, when I got back to it, found that personal belongings including my camera had been taken. If I claim for this theft, will I lose my no-claim bonus?

A: It varies from insurance company to insurance company so you must check with your insurers and look carefully at the terms of your policy. Even if, strictly, your no-claim bonus could be affected by making a claim, your insurance company has a discretion in the matter if it considers you to have been completely blameless.

Q: My father has died and I find he has left substantial debts on three credit cards. Must these be paid out of his estate?

A: Yes. Credit card debts are the same as any other debts outstanding when a person dies and must be settled in the same way.

Q: I saw a lovely garden furniture set in the department store which announced interest-free credit. I decided to buy it on easy monthly instalments. However, I was turned down. I've been trying to find out what the problem is but I can't get any satisfaction. I seem to be on some sort of credit blacklist but, although I've bought lots of things on hire purchase in the past, I've never been in arrears or defaulted on payment. How can I find out what has happened?

A: This store, or indeed any organisation which offers credit is not legally obliged to tell you why you have been refused credit but there is a good chance that a refusal has been based upon information received by them from a credit reference agency.

You can demand to know which credit reference agency has supplied the information about your credit standing and they are obliged to give you the name and address within 28 days of your application to buy the furniture on credit. You should then write to the agency, who, in turn, must supply you with a copy of your recorded details and may charge a small fee. If no details are known, the agency must tell you that also.

The credit reference agency holds information ranging from a record of subscribers who have requested credit details about you, together with transactions in which you have been involved with your prior record of payment, to any outstanding county court judgments. In Scotland, decrees replace judgments.

If you do not agree with the information recorded under your name, you can require the agency to remove or amend its records – stating your reasons in full – and the agency is bound by law to respond within 28 days. If the agency fails to respond or amend its records you can send a 'notice of correction', which should be a clear explanation of why you believe the entry needs altering. Your local Citizens' Advice Bureau can help you draft the note if necessary. The note then has to be added to the file. However, this is not the end of the story if you are not satisfied. You are further entitled under the Consumer Credit Act 1974 to write to the Director General of Fair Trading, Field House, Bream's Buildings, London EC4A 1PR, setting out your grievances over the incorrect entry, and this office will contact the agency on your behalf and investigate your complaint.

If you see or believe there is a judgment or decree entered against you, and if this had now been satisfied, you are well advised to apply to the court concerned for a 'certificate of satisfaction', which for a £1 fee will be issued by the Public Registry and will result in the removal from public records of any unpaid judgment. A copy of this will be sent to the credit reference agencies, who will record that judgment has been satisfied. In Scotland there is no equivalent procedure for the registration of 'satisfaction' as just described, but if you can provide suitable evidence that payment has been made, your file will indicate that the decree has been paid.

Finally, if you want to make a general enquiry as to your credit standing, we have listed several credit data agencies at the end of the book to whom you can write.

If you wish to make sure that all national records relating to your credit-worthiness are accurate you should contact Registry Trust Limited, 173–175 Cleveland Street, London W1P 5PE.

Q: My boyfriend and I are planning to buy a house together. I want us to marry but he says we can get a better mortgage if we don't. Is he right?

A: Name the day! Since August 1988 there is no advantage to be gained by a couple each retaining their single status to obtain the tax relief on a mortgage. So, no excuses for reluctant brides or bridegrooms – married or single, two can live as cheaply as two!

9. DANGER – WOMEN AT WORK!

We've always found that a little light flirtation with a male colleague can make the day – if not our hearts – go faster. But, sadly, there are some men who can be positive nuisances and use their position to cause embarrassment or hold a woman back. What can be done about them?

Q: My boss asked me to work late and, as I need the money, I was grateful for the offer. Unfortunately, he made a pass at me. I managed to put him off fairly pleasantly but I'm rather nervous. I need the extra cash and he has implied I'll lose my job and not just the overtime if I don't do what he wants. Have I any legal rights?

A: You do have rights and if, in spite of your protests, your boss continues his threats, forcing you to leave your job, you might be able to make an application to an industrial tribunal on the grounds of unfair dismissal, depending on your length of time in the job and the size of your employer's workforce. You must make an application within three months of the termination of your employment. No legal aid is available for such an application so in the first instance you might seek advice from ACAS. You can also refer to the Equal Opportunities Commission or the National Council for Civil Liberties.

Q: I work for a large organisation and the chance for promotion came up recently. Four of us were shortlisted – the other three were men. The man who got the job is not as good as I am; his qualifications are not as good as mine and I know I'm just as good as he is at staff relations. Is there anything I can do about this?

A: The sex discrimination legislation makes it positively unlawful for a woman, otherwise qualified for a post, to be passed over on the grounds of sex. You can attempt to seek justice by applying to the industrial tribunal, who can rule upon the practices of your employer and award you compensation if your application is successful. All the same rules as to time limits and legal aid apply as in the previous answer and an approach to the bodies mentioned is recommended.

However, you must weigh the fact that you might get a reputation as a troublemaker. Unfair? Yes. But it might be worth having a discussion about your future with your present employers to assess their attitude. And keep an eye out for openings with a firm which practises what the Sexual Discrimination Act preaches!

Q: I'm a heavy smoker and now the firm I work for has announced that they are banning smoking from the office. We've taken it to mean that if we don't obey the ruling, we will be fired or have to resign. Are they within their rights in doing this?

A: It seems they are. A man who brought a claim

DANGER – WOMEN AT WORK! 99

against his employers recently, stating that a smoking ban amounted to constructive dismissal, had his case dismissed by an industrial tribunal. This ruling conflicted with a 1984 industrial tribunal decision but since the medical evidence that passive smoking – i.e. breathing in other people's smoke – can be a health hazard, it is felt that similar bans are justified on medical grounds.

Before the ban is introduced, your employers should talk to the staff and perhaps arrange a smoking area where nicotine addicts can light up in their breaks.

However, we would point out that resigning or being fired are not the only choices. You could give up smoking. Think of the money you'd save and how well you would feel!

Q: My daughter has been working for a double-glazing company for two years and last week she was sacked without warning. She was told that the company could not afford to keep her and she is shocked and distraught because of the hard work and effort she had put into her job. She was taken on as a self-employed worker and she does not know how she stands with regard to her tax or stamp position. Her boss had told her not to worry about this. Can she claim compensation for unfair dismissal?

A: If your daughter was self-employed then she cannot claim for unfair dismissal as an employed person can. However, she can claim for a period of notice to which she would be entitled under any agreement she had made with the company, or, in the absence of such agreement, the law will imply a reasonable period of notice. Her tax and stamp are her own responsibility as a self-employed person but she can seek advice from her local tax office to see whether the company properly classified her as self-employed. Depending on her duties, she might be considered by the Inland Revenue as an employed person for whose tax and stamp the company had a liability to pay.

Q: I was a member of an amateur writers' circle. The leader of the group was a very nice man who had had short stories published in various magazines and was working on his second novel. He'd had one published some years previously although it hadn't been a particular success. One of the exercises he gave the class was to invent titles for different genres. I came up with a rather good thriller title. Now I see that his second novel is to be published and it has my title. I'm furious as I wanted to use it myself some time and, even if I hadn't, he hasn't asked my permission. Is there anything I can do?

A: Frustrating and annoying though it is, there is no copyright in titles. In any event, you positively volunteered this title for general consumption when you evidently could not resist displaying your talent in this class exercise. What a pity for you that you didn't get your book written first. We're sure that you will think up an even better title in time – but keep it to yourself!

One thing you could do, though, is inform fellow members of your circle of what he has done. And if the circle is organised by a local education authority, tell them. He deserves it!

Q: Last year I got a job as a manager in a bakery firm. My basic wage was for a ten-hour shift, five nights a week, but gradually I was expected to work longer hours with no extra pay. I said nothing as I was anxious to keep the job, which I enjoyed. However, one morning I was taken ill just before I left for work and my husband called my employers to let them know I couldn't get to work. My boss reacted aggressively and was abusive to my husband before slamming down the phone. The next day when I complained about my employer's rudeness I was told bluntly that if I didn't like it I could go. I was upset and did leave, but to date my ex-boss has refused to pay my outstanding wages. I would like to recover the money due, which is only £84, but I am worried about the legal costs involved in any claim.

A: You must feel aggrieved at what has happened. At minimal costs you can seek a recovery of the sums owed by using the 'small claims' procedure through your local county court. However, you might be entitled to claim unfair dismissal at the industrial tribunal, or even wrongful dismissal through the courts. But the full facts of your case would have to be considered and we strongly urge you to seek competent legal advice, beginning perhaps at your local law centre.

Q: I work four afternoons a week. Do I have the same job rights as someone working full time?

A: As a general guide, you have the same rights if you work at least sixteen hours a week. For instance, if you have worked in the same job for sixteen hours a week for two years, your employer cannot fire you without good reason. And, no matter how many hours a week you put in, some legal rights apply to all employees. These include the right not to be discriminated against because of your race or sex, or victimised for trade union activities.

Q: My daughter has recently been sacked from her job with a large company with whom she has been employed for over four years. She believes she was unfairly dismissed and is waiting for the outcome of the company appeal procedure before applying to the industrial tribunal. Is this a sensible course of action or is she in danger of any prejudice to her position?

A: Any person qualifying for application to the industrial tribunal (and this appears to include your daughter) *must* apply within three months from the date of dismissal. Generally, anything short of being in a certified coma would appear to be insufficient grounds for an extension to this deadline. Your daughter should put in her application without delay and irrespective of internal procedures. This is a straightforward process and it can be simply withdrawn if your daughter's appeal succeeds.

Q: My husband was injured at work when the head of a new hammer, supplied by his employers, flew off and struck him heavily on the foot. He went to the foreman, who told him that as the hammer was purchased elsewhere, my husband had to sue the suppliers of the hammer for any compensation. Does he really have to do this?

A: No, he does not. Since the Employers' Liability (Defective Equipment) Act 1969, any employee injured by defective equipment in the course of his employment can look directly to his employers for damages. His employers might have a claim against the suppliers but that is their decision and does not affect their liability to your husband.

Q: As pensioners, my friends and I have often attended our local town hall, which organises tea dances. When I last went I was crossing the dance floor when I slipped and fell and my wrist was broken. A lot of people had noticed the floor was unusually slippery and complained about it that afternoon, describing it as an 'ice rink', but the council have refused to pay me any compensation – saying a dance floor has to be highly polished and it was up to me to take care. Is there any point in pursuing a claim?

A: Yes, there is. Whilst the floors do have to be suitably polished for dancing, a line is drawn where a floor is so slippery as to create an obvious danger – or where perhaps patches of polish may have been inadequately buffed so that hazard areas are created. If you have supporting witnesses as to the unusually slippery condition of the floor then you could well show that on that afternoon the council had negligently created a danger for those people, including yourself, who might be expected to be using the floor that day.

Q: I have a job which I thoroughly enjoy. By coincidence, I work alongside a man who shares the same date of birth. Now I'm coming up to retirement and he has five years to go. I don't want to! Is it legal for me to be compulsorily retired while my colleague isn't?

A: Good to hear of a woman who's happy in her work! The European Court has ruled that a woman is legally entitled to work until she reaches 65 if she so wishes, and this ruling is binding upon all member states of the EEC. Therefore you can retire at 60 or keep at it for another five years if you so wish.

Q: I've been working part-time for a company for nearly three years now. I was married six months ago and we are talking of starting a family. If we do, I'd like to go back to my job and I'm wondering what my position is regarding length of leave and pay. I work a twenty-hour week.

A: You clearly qualify for maternity leave and pay in view of the length and hours of your employment, which exceeds two years with the same employer and more than sixteen hours per week. You will be entitled to claim maternity leave and the right to return to the same job, as long as you inform your employer that you intend to exercise this right. You should give notice that you are taking maternity leave and of your intention to return at least 21 days before you in fact leave work. If you change your mind about going back to work you can inform your employer after the birth and likewise you must give notice to your employer at least three weeks before you intend to resume your job.

You are entitled to a legal maximum of 40 weeks leave, that is, at least 11 weeks before the birth and up to 29 weeks after, although both you and your employer can postpone your return for up to a further four weeks if you have medical grounds and your employer, for his part, gives proper reasons.

Maternity leave does not count as a period of absence from work for any purpose and on your return you are entitled to be treated as if you had not been away, taking advantage of pay rises and rights not to be unfairly dismissed.

If you are not offered your own job or an equivalent alternative on your return, you can take your employer to the industrial tribunal, to which he will have to justify his actions.

Whilst on maternity leave you will be entitled to Statutory Maternity Pay, if you have paid National Insurance Contributions, which allows you up to 90 per cent of your earnings for six weeks followed by 12 weeks at a lower rate. This lower rate is set by the government and can change (currently it is around £36.25 per week) and it is also payable for a period of up to 18 weeks for women who have worked for at least six months up to and including the fifteenth week before the baby is due.

Finally, do check the position with your employer (or union representative) and your own contract of employment as you might find that your company provides even better arrangements for leave and pay than those described above, which are, of course, set down as a minimum entitlement under the law.

DANGER – WOMEN AT WORK!

Q: I am a self-employed, divorced woman and I employ a nanny for my six-year-old son. She is absolutely essential to me and my career. Can I claim a proportion of her earnings against tax?

A: No. Although the nanny is employed to enable you to work in the first place, the Inland Revenue will not allow any part of her pay to be offset against your tax as they consider her duties to be entirely domestic and therefore separate and unconnected with your actual work.

If the nanny also acts partly as your secretary, then you may well be able to claim part of her wages as business expenditure.

Q: I have got the most adorable baby daughter. I took maternity leave (on full pay) to have her, fully intending to go back to my job. Now I just don't want to but I'm worried. I know they won't have any problems replacing me but will I have to pay back the money I've had?

A: Congratulations. Nice to know you're nappy-happy! You certainly do not have to repay any monies to which you would have been entitled as Statutory Maternity Pay, as you would have received that whether or not you later decided to return to work.

However, if you have received more than the Statutory Maternity Pay by arrangement with your employer, then whether or not you have to repay the extra amount depends upon the exact terms upon which this was paid to you. If you were paid upon condition of your return to work, your employer may demand repayment of the extra amount from you.

10. HOME SWEET HOME

How pleasant it would be to close the door and just relax and forget about the cares of the world. Unfortunately, an Englishman's home – not to mention any woman's – is not always a castle. And if it were, we'd still want to pull up the drawbridge against rapacious landlords, cowboy builders, tiresome tenants and door-to-door salesmen.

Q: We have just bought our house and are wondering what, legally, we can expect to find as fixtures and fittings when we move in.

A: This is something which ought to form part of your contract with your seller. Legally, he must leave behind anything that cannot be removed without causing serious damage to the building or land to which it is attached. Apart from that he can take out everything that he has not already agreed will remain and which has not been included in the sale price. If nothing is said about fixtures and fittings in the contract or sale negotiations, then you may find yourself in the same position as a friend of ours who arrived at her newly bought flat in the dark to find the vendor had taken everything, down to the last light bulb. Not exactly the brightest of homecomings. However, the vendor was in breach of the law of generosity only, not in breach of contract.

Q: My husband and I recently found a flat which we liked and felt we could just afford to buy. We made an offer which was accepted, instructed solicitors, obtained an offer of a mortgage and sent a surveyor for a check. Imagine our disappointment and frustration when we discovered that the owner of the flat had sold to another couple at a higher price! Now we find that we have bills from the solicitors and the surveyor. Is there any way we can claim these expenses from the owner? After all, he led us to believe that we were going to purchase his property.

A: What you have described is the classic case of gazumping in England and Wales, a disgraceful practice that is unfortunately so common that the word now appears in the dictionary. It adds insult to injury to be let down in this way and then face legal and other bills on top. Unfortunately, in nearly all cases, when you agree to buy a property in England and Wales you have no legal relationship with the seller until contracts are actually exchanged – hence the phrase 'subject to contract' whenever property is offered for sale. We would love to say otherwise but, sorry, this is one time when the law simply cannot help you. In Scotland, however, there is a greater measure of protection for both buyer and seller. If a formal, written offer is made for a property and is accepted unconditionally in a prescribed written form, then neither party can opt out of the agreement simply because the price, after all, doesn't suit either one of them.

Q: I rent my flat which is one of a number in a small block. I and the other tenants heard that the landlord who owns the block was negotiating to sell it and we have met together and decided that, as a group, we would like to buy his interest. We approached the landlord but have met with no response. Surely this landlord cannot sell above our heads if we have shown that we wish to be considered as purchasers; and if he does sell to an outside party, is there anything we could do?

A: If your landlord does sell to an outside party, he could well be in breach of a brand new law which allows tenants far greater rights than they previously had. The Landlord and Tenant Act 1987 (England and Wales) gives tenants in your position a first option to buy their landlord's interest, assuming proper terms and conditions can be agreed. If the landlord fails to offer his interest to the tenants and sells elsewhere, they can require the purchaser to resell the interest on the terms on which he bought. As with all matters affecting property, you should seek professional guidance on how the new legislation works, which parts of the Act are actually in force and, just as important, the best way of securing a good deal for all of you if the law permits and you decide to assert your rights to buy.

Q: As my husband was coming down the stairs carrying a pot of paint (bright yellow, unfortunately), he tripped and the paint went all over the stair carpet and also on to his good trousers. He wasn't decorating at the time, just transporting the paint from upstairs to the kitchen. Try as we have, we cannot remove the stains. I have a new-for-old household contents policy. Can I claim on it?

A: The small print of your insurance policy will tell you whether you can successfully claim for your newly painted carpet and trousers or whether you

HOME SWEET HOME

will have to live with partially bright yellow stairs, passing them off as 'art nouveau'!

Only if your policy gives you full accidental damage cover will you be able to claim. Most household policies give only limited protection for television, video and glass damage, and this would not be enough to restore carpets or trousers to their former glory.

Q: While I was away for the weekend a couple of months ago, my flat was broken into and burgled. I sorted things out with my insurers but now my telephone bill has come and I'm horrified to see that it's about £250 more than usual. When I checked, I discovered that on the weekend in question, calls were made from my flat to America and Australia and heaven knows where else. I explained this to British Telecom but they say that I have to pay, and if I don't I'll be cut off and have to pay a re-connection charge if I want the phone restored. The police have not caught the burglars. Will I really have to pay this bill? I don't have that kind of money to spare but I do need a telephone.

A: It adds insult to injury to discover that not only has your home been violated but the burglars also took time to make several calls overseas – at your expense. Regrettably, there is little you can do but pay up if you want to hang on to your telephone. Check back with your insurers, but we doubt that you will be covered for this loss. However, you might think it worth telling the police. If British Telecom has a record of the calls, they might also have a record of the numbers called. The police might be able to find out who received the calls and, from them, the identity of the caller.

Q: We moved into our new bungalow and discovered to our horror that we could hear every word spoken in the bungalow next door, which is linked to ours at bedroom level. The council's building inspectors confirmed that the builder had contravened building regulations and forced him to make amends. There are no problems now with noise but the builder has refused to compensate us for any stress and disturbance, and we have lost some space in a bedroom and the bathroom because of the sound-proofing. Do you think we are eligible for some compensation?

A: Well, at least he's brought you and your neighbours into close contact! Seriously, though, we think you are owed compensation. The builder's contract with you contains an implied guarantee that the building regulations have been complied with and you should be compensated for anything you suffer by his breach of that clause.

Your best bet is to bring a small claims action in your local county or sheriff's court. You don't need a solicitor for this but your local Citizens' Advice Bureau can advise and help.

Q: We bought our dream flat two months ago. It's only now that we are moving in and, to our horror, some of our furniture doesn't fit. The estate agent gave us a ground plan of the flat with measurements filled in and I'm afraid we didn't bother to measure up ourselves. Now we find our settee and dining table are too large for the rooms. My husband rang the estate agent and he just said the measurements were approximate, meant only as a guideline. Do we have any case against him? Our furniture is quite expensive as well as being what we like.

A: Well, this is a word of warning to everyone not to take anything on trust when it comes to buying a property and to double-check everything yourself. Advice that's a little late for you, unfortunately. Estate agents normally have exclusion clauses on their particulars which prevent would-be purchasers placing reliance upon the contents.

You have described a ground plan, however, which you may have been entitled to rely upon, but it will be hard indeed for you to claim against the agent when you had every opportunity to check the measurements. Besides, from what you've said, it seems that you already had the furniture before you bought the flat: you did not buy the furniture relying on the measurements. You certainly do not seem to have any claim against the agent in respect of your purchase of the flat.

Q: I have been pestered for the last couple of weeks by obscene phone calls. The caller obviously knows quite a lot about me and, although I've never done anything really outrageous, I wouldn't like people to know about certain things in my past – which is what this man threatens. I called the police but they say they can do nothing about such phone calls and can only act if there is a physical assault. They were very sympathetic and suggested I might change my phone number, but I don't want to do this as it would involve me in a lot of bother and maybe a loss of work as I work from home. Is it really true that the police can do nothing in such cases?

A: Unfortunately, the police are correct, although if you were actually being threatened with physical harm, this would itself constitute an assault and a criminal offence upon which the police could act – if they knew who to arrest. Likewise, if you knew the identity of the caller you could bring a civil action against him, which would result in an injunction to stop this legal 'nuisance'.

As it is, the only solutions would be to a) do nothing and hope the caller gets tired of his stupid antics, and b) change your number – but if it's a business phone you can hardly go ex-directory and therefore you gain little from this option, and c) contact British Telecom, who might agree to monitor and intervene on your calls, which is the most likely and satisfactory course in your case.

Q: Our cleaning lady slipped and fell on our rather highly polished floor last week. Fortunately, she was perfectly all right, especially after a glass of sherry! But it did set me wondering as to what the position is if a cleaner or window-cleaner has an accident in my home. Would I be liable?

A: If a visitor to your home has an accident (and a visitor includes any person who lawfully comes to your house) then there is a potential liability for any injury or loss suffered. However, you would only be liable if the injury is caused by some negligence on your part, and your household insurance policy may well cover you for this type of situation. If you have such a policy – read it!

Q: We live in a council house and an elderly visitor tripped over on the path leading to our front door. The path was broken up by council workmen when they were doing works to pipes below the front garden and, despite our numerous complaints, they failed to reinstate the paving. As we occupy the house and the path leads to our premises, does our visitor have any claim against us or can she sue the council for her injury?

A: The council normally retain control over the structure and outsides of their properties. If, as is likely, they had an obligation to maintain and repair premises they let, then your visitor would certainly have a claim against them for their failure to meet their obligation in respect of the path, especially as you had actually complained about it.

HOME SWEET HOME

Q: My husband and I applied for and received an improvement grant from our local authority. The grant covered most of the cost of damp-proofing and wood treatment for our home. The problem is that the builders who carried out the work did not, in our opinion, do a good job and further work (and money) may be needed. The local authority officer nevertheless authorised payment to the builders, who have since gone into liquidation. Do we have any claim against the local authority as by approving the payments they appeared to have also approved the work?

A: There is no easy answer to this, but the courts have recently decided that generally there is no liability on a local authority in respect of improvement grants since there is no duty of care to the person who receives the grant. Such a stance is justified because of the lack of control, in real terms, that the local authority had over your builders, who were at all times a party to a contract with you or your husband.

Q: My husband has been offered the opportunity to work abroad for at least a year. We are considering renting out our flat whilst we are away, but I am concerned that we would have difficulty in getting the flat back from tenants when we return to England.

A: If the flat has been your residence prior to the letting, then you would be entitled to possession of the property upon your return. We strongly advise, however, that you seek expert help in drawing up any tenancy agreement so as to ensure that you don't come home to problems.

Q: We have recently bought a house and upon moving in we told the estate agents to take down their sign. They did so last week, but as it had been nailed to weatherboarding at the front of the house, several slats appear to be quite seriously damaged where the sign was ripped off. Do we have any recourse and, if so, against whom?

A: Your question raises a number of possible answers: first, if you are quite sure that the damage was caused by the removal of the sign, you could look to the estate agent for compensation. If, on the other hand, the *erection* of the sign was the cause of damage, you would have a possible claim against both the agents and the former house owners only if the sign was put up after exchange of contracts. Any damage occurring before this crucial time would leave you with no remedy since you are deemed to buy the house as you find it.

Q: In June we bought a property and since moving in we have had nothing but problems: the ceilings in the bedrooms have come down; there is rising damp and the house smells musty. Our health is suffering and our lives are a misery owing to the condition of the house. We purchased the house with a mortgage from the building society, who had a survey carried out, but we were told nothing of the faults which must have been obvious. We are not eligible for a local authority grant and have no money to rectify the problems. Have we any remedy against the surveyor?

A: You certainly would have a remedy against the surveyor but only if you can show that he was negligent and failed to account for obvious faults when he carried out the survey. We strongly urge you to seek advice from a solicitor but be warned – even if you succeed, your recovery may not cover the cost of the repairs and you could still be out of pocket.

Q: Is there anything I can do about the persistent parking outside my house? Often the same cars appear and sometimes my garage entrance is blocked, although for the most part the vehicles are positioned so as to make it as awkward as possible for me to get my own car in and out of the drive.

A: Apart from heartfelt sympathy we can offer precious little comfort. If you reside on a designated public highway you can do nothing to stop legitimate parking, however awkward it may be for you. However, if you find your drive actually blocked, this does constitute an actionable obstruction and your local police may well assist in finding the offender and even prosecute. If you want to resort to it, you can bring a civil action for nuisance against persistent and known 'blockers'. A cautionary tale here: a fellow sufferer complained vociferously to the local council, who 'helpfully' responded by painting yellow lines all down his road; both he and the neighbours wished he had endured it in silence.

Q: For the past three years I have been a tenant occupying the ground-floor flat of a house. I have just found out that the landlord has defaulted on his mortgage to the building society, who are seeking possession through the court of the whole property. The mortgage, it seems, was granted last year and my landlord 'forgot' to tell them of my tenancy. I seem to be facing eviction and am desperate – is there anything I can do?

A: Yes, and you should make your position known quickly! Inform the building society of your tenancy and how long you have been there. Find out from them the date of the court action and go along there on the day as an 'intervening party', i.e. one affected by an order likely to be made. On the facts here, you look to have full protection as the mortgage was given after your tenancy and the building society cannot now gain vacant possession of the property. The position would be very different if your tenancy had commenced after the mortgage had been granted. In your case, it would seem that you cannot be evicted, and if the property is sold you remain the tenant with a new and, hopefully, more scrupulous landlord.

Q: We had builders in to erect an extension to the back of our house but halfway through the work they simply abandoned us. We made enquiries and discovered that the company had gone into liquidation, and we have now had estimates of twice the price to finish the job. Where do we stand?

A: Regrettably, you stand right in the middle of an expensive mess. Unfortunately for you, if the company is no longer operating then there is little point in pursuing them. Find out if a receiver has been appointed and, if so, whether there is any chance that he is managing any works for the company. In that case, you can entreat him to get your extension completed. If not, then you will just have to pay up or live with a half-finished extension. You may think it worthwhile to lodge a claim with the liquidator in the hope of recovering some of the increased cost of the work.

Q: We have rented a flat but the landlord insisted that we sign a document describing the letting as a 'licence'. There is no fixed term for our letting and the flat is self-contained, but we are concerned that by signing this document, the landlord can evict us at any time without good reason.

A: A tenancy by any other name is still a tenancy! If you have exclusive possession of the flat and there is no provision for the landlord to have unrestricted access to the premises, then you almost certainly have the full protection of tenants under the Rent Acts and calling your letting a 'licence' is but a transparent attempt by the landlord to get around your rights. If you have any doubts about your tenure, take your letting agreement to your local Citizens' Advice Bureau or law centre. They will undoubtedly settle the matter for you.

Q: Is there anything I can do to prevent any future owners of my house from tearing down ivy which houses a wren's nest or from cutting down a delightful cherry blossom tree? I am thinking of moving but I would like to feel that these items are protected if I sell up.

A: You might be able to persuade a buyer of your home to enter an agreement, as a special condition of sale, not to interfere with either the ivy or the tree. However, such an agreement could affect the sale price of your property or even put off a purchaser altogether, and in any case it would not bind any subsequent purchaser of the house. Sometimes the local authority will put preservation orders on certain trees to prevent them being cut down but we doubt that they would put such an order on a cherry blossom tree.

Q: A huge lime tree is growing on the pavement outside my house and I am sure it is causing structural damage to the house as well as depriving us of daylight. The local council refuses to fell. What can I do about it?

A: If the tree is simply depriving you of daylight, you have no remedy. If, however, you have good reason to believe that your property is being adversely affected then you should first seek expert advice from a surveyor. If your suspicions turn out to be accurate and the tree is causing or likely to cause damage, you may be able to take court action against the council, requiring them to fell it. If damage has already been caused, the council may well be liable for the cost of remedial work but you will need detailed legal advice to pursue that one.

Q: We bought an eighteenth century cottage this year and had the walls injected against damp and then plastered. Unfortunately, the damp has seeped through and the surveyor says this is because the builder used the wrong plaster. The builder, for his part, says we didn't let the plaster dry out properly and absolutely refuses to do the work without further payment. Can we rely on the surveyor's report and force the builder to do the work at no more cost to us, or will we have to employ another firm?

A: You can certainly rely on the surveyor's report but if the builder still refuses to provide his services without charge, you can't force him to carry out any extra work. What you can do is to get another builder and then use the surveyor and his report as the basis of a claim against the first builder to recover the cost of redoing the work – if it is proved and accepted that it was defective work in the first place, as your surveyor believes.

Q: Some months ago my husband and I bought an old cottage in the country which had some outbuildings erected before we moved in. Now our neighbours are complaining that one of the walls of the outbuildings is responsible for cracking their sewer pipe and this has led to rats entering their garden. The outbuildings were not put up by us and frankly we don't even use them. Can we be held responsible for what is happening?

A: And you thought you escaped the rat race when you moved to the country! Problems seem to crop up everywhere and this one could well be your responsibility if the damage to the pipe has occurred since you purchased the cottage. You will have to try to find out discreetly or otherwise if any similar

HOME SWEET HOME

complaint by your neighbours was being made before you bought the cottage. That would be one way of establishing that the problem existed before you moved in. If it can be shown that damage was caused before your purchase of the cottage, the previous owner could well be responsible to your neighbours. In any event, whenever the damage occurred, you might be able to recover any loss from him – depending upon whether he gave accurate and full answers to enquiries made by your solicitors when you bought the property.

You need expert advice here – from both a solicitor and a surveyor – and you should have a close look at your insurance position.

Q: We live in a rented flat which is one of a number in a large converted house. For months now we have endured constant flooding from our toilet, which is unpleasant as well as creating mess and aggravation every time it occurs. The fault lies somewhere in the pipes which serve all the flats, and it seems that attention needs to be given to the plumbing in the flat upstairs before our problem is cured. We know this because, despite telephone calls, personal visits and letters, our landlord, who is responsible for all such repairs as this, has ignored us and we ended up paying for a plumber ourselves, but he was unable to cure the problem. We are at our wits' end and we wonder whether to resort to sending a solicitor's letter to the landlord to make him act. This is expensive, but if it brings results it will be worth it. We don't know what else we can do!

A: A landlord like yours would be just as likely to ignore a solicitor's letter – however expensive – as he has ignored your letters and calls. An order obtained by you in your local county or sheriff's court is much more likely to achieve the desired response and you can seek assistance from either the court office or, better still, your local law centre or Citizens' Advice Bureau.

Have you thought of having a word with the occupier upstairs? If he, too, is a tenant he might join forces with you against the landlord. He might even clear up the faulty plumbing himself or pay for or towards the cost of your plumber to do the work – so you will at least know it's done. You can claim the cost from your landlord if he was indeed obliged to carry out the repairs under the terms of your tenancy agreement.

11. NO FIXED ABODE

Some questions do not fit naturally into any category. So, if you've not spotted your particular problem anywhere else in this book, you might find the answer here. We hope so.

Q: My elderly mother was attacked in the street. Her handbag was snatched and she was knocked to the ground. She was shocked and bruised, and because she landed on her face her nose was broken and her lip badly cut. Her attacker has not been caught but, even so, is there any chance of her receiving some compensation for this attack from the police or some government body?

A: Yes, there is a body from which your poor mother can claim well-deserved compensation. It is called the Criminal Injuries Compensation Board, and if you write to them at 19 Alfred Place, Chenies Street, London WC1E 7LG (or in Scotland at Blythswood House, 200 West Regent Street, Glasgow G2 4SW) they will send you details of how to apply for compensation. If you and your mother have any problems with the leaflets or forms, we are sure your local Citizens' Advice Bureau or law centre will be glad to help. They will advise whether your mother's injuries qualify for an award, as a minimum for compensation exists.

Q: Reading about people dressing up as policemen and attacking lonely women on motorways and elsewhere, I feel very worried. If I am stopped in my car and I don't think it's by genuine policemen and drive off, what happens if they *are* genuine? Can I be taken to court for obstructing the police in the course of their duty? It is very worrying.

A: Yes, it is. This also applies to men who come to the door claiming to be gas or electricity meter readers. In these cases, if you're not expecting them, you can close the door and ring the appropriate office to see whether they are genuine. We would advise this, as it's better to spend a little time and be overcautious. However, back to the motorway. Every police officer should carry a warrant card, and you can and should insist on seeing it to satisfy yourself that the person in question is a police officer. Whilst an impersonator might get hold of a uniform, you can feel fairly certain that the holder of a warrant card is the authentic article and entitled to your co-operation. If you do drive off in the face of a genuine request from the police to stop, you could find yourself falling foul of the law. On the other hand, if you have a real doubt as to the identity of the persons who stop you, you may be wise to drive off – but play safe by reporting to a police station at the first opportunity.

Q: I've just been fined for speeding – I was about four miles per hour over the limit. Fair enough. But I've just read of a case in the next town where a culprit who exceeded the limit by twenty miles an hour has been fined less than I. Not fair! Why aren't transgressions like this treated equally, with everyone being fined the same for a first offence and then more – but equally – for any further offence?

A: In the system of British justice you can be absolutely certain of the sentence in respect of murder, which carries life, at one end of the spectrum and, at the other end, fixed penalties, e.g. for parking on a yellow line. In between, there are theoretically as many variations as there are courts and, although judges and magistrates are given guidelines and tariffs, it is sometimes the luck of the draw. True, it can seem unfair – but if a sentence seems wildly out you can appeal to a higher court.

Q: Having completed my shopping in the local supermarket, I was leaving my car-parking space when I was confronted by a runaway trolley which damaged my car. I immediately saw the manager, who said he was unable to do anything. However, if I now make a claim on my insurance I risk losing my no-claim bonus. Can I hold the supermarket responsible?

A: Oh, those demon trollies! We sympathise, but you would only have a claim against the supermarket if you could show that the damage to your car was caused by fault on the part of the supermarket or its staff – for example, if the trolley area was on a slope which allowed unsecured trollies to run, unchecked, across the car park; or if a member of the staff had pushed the trolley into the path of your car. Without this kind of evidence you would find it hard to succeed in a claim against the supermarket, who would *not* be liable for the negligence of its customers.

Q: There have been a lot of attacks on women and three rapes in my area over the last six months. When I was on holiday in France, I bought a cylinder of gas which I plan to use if any man attacks me. However, my friend says they are illegal (I bought it quite openly in France) and that, if I used it, I could be prosecuted. Surely if I used it in self-defence, it would not be an offence? How is a woman supposed to protect herself?

A: Good question! Karate, judo, handbags and umbrellas appear to be the expected tools of trade in self-defence for women. Gas cylinders are definitely not on the list, any more than knives, guns or knuckle-dusters.

Anything that is designated as a weapon is generally considered offensive and is illegal to carry in Britain, even if intended for defensive purposes only.

Perhaps less devastating and more feeble in its effect than a gas cylinder, but a perfume spray aimed well at its target might be some measure of use – and a whistle is always handy!

Q: How far is a woman entitled to go to defend herself against an assault? I've taken to carrying a small knife with me as I live in a dodgy area, but a friend says I could be charged if I wounded someone even in self-defence.

A: If you are attacked in your home or in the street, you are entitled to use any reasonable force to ward off the attack. This can include the use of a weapon to hand such as a kitchen knife or heavy object but, as we have seen, you cannot actually carry a knife or other weapon with you in a public place as this is an illegal act – even if, perversely, its use might be legitimate self-defence in certain circumstances.

The use of reasonable force is also permitted if you intervene on behalf of someone that you see being attacked.

NO FIXED ABODE

Q: I was raped four months ago. I got home, closed the door and did nothing about it. I was so shocked and I just couldn't face anyone – not the doctor, the police, my family. Now I've come to terms with it. I read a case in the local paper about another victim and I'm sure it's the same man. I can't help feeling guilty because if I'd reported it, this man could have been stopped. Is it too late for me to report it now? If I do, will I have to go to court?

A: First of all, don't blame yourself for a perfectly natural reaction. Few people feel like going through an ordeal twice by having to report the crime as well as suffering it. But, as you point out, only by reporting crimes can the perpetrators be stopped, and you will find the police very sympathetic.

It is never *too* late to report any crime, although it is right to say the earlier a crime is reported the greater the chance the police have of catching a criminal and securing a conviction. As for going to court, it is generally necessary and expected that the victim of a crime gives evidence about it, particularly in the area of physical assault including rape. If, however, there is evidence apart from your testimony that would seem sufficient to secure a conviction, then you might just be able to avoid having to relive this episode by going to court.

Q: I got up from my seat on the bus as it was approaching my stop. It lurched suddenly and I was flung to the ground. I told the conductor I was going to make a complaint. He said that the rules are that you should only get up when the bus has stopped. I took his number and the bus's number, but because of what he said, did nothing about it. My friend was with me at the time. Now, two years later, my knee still hurts and the doctor says I've developed arthritis which might have been caused by a fall in the past. Is there anything I can do? Quite frankly, if I had waited for the bus to stop before getting up, it would have started up again before I reached the exit. And, anyway, suppose I had been a standing passenger?

A: If indeed you had been a standing passenger and fallen when the bus lurched to avoid a car in its path, you would have no comeback unless you could show negligence on the part of the bus driver. There lies the problem. To succeed in any such claim, you need to show the bus driver was at fault, and since you have to prove your claim it would not be enough merely to show the bus jerked and you fell.

The fact that you got up to get off before the bus stopped would not in itself be a bar to a claim in negligence (if negligence can be proved).

After this passage of time your chance of success is remote, but since you have three years to bring a claim it might be worth writing to the bus company – but don't hold out too much hope.

Q: My car was badly damaged recently when it was struck by a fire engine which had jumped the lights on its way, apparently, to answer an emergency call. I have been told that I will not recover the cost of repairs to my car as the fire engine had the right of way at the traffic lights, even though I crossed the lights showing green in my favour. Is this correct?

A: Any vehicle answering an emergency does not automatically have a right of way at controlled junctions, including traffic lights. They do not have to comply with traffic signs or signals if they take reasonable care to see that it is safe to proceed. You may well have a claim if you can show that the firemen failed to take reasonable care when they crossed the lights and hit your car.

Q: My husband and I have recently returned from our

holiday abroad which was ruined for us by the non-arrival of our luggage until two days before we were due to come home. Although we managed to buy some clothing and toiletries, we were basically without decent holiday clothes for the entire fortnight. The tension of waiting each day on the off chance that our suitcase would arrive, and the frustration of hardly managing with what we had, spoilt the entire trip. We have been offered a paltry sum by way of compensation from the tour operators, but I think we should have all our money back. Are we entitled to this?

A: We really feel for you and wish we would tell you that you can recover the entire cost of your disappointing holiday. Regrettably, you are only entitled to the costs of the essential items purchased whilst waiting for your luggage to arrive, plus a reasonable amount to compensate for your distress and inconvenience. This amount would not, we fear, meet anything like the cost of your holiday, but hopefully it would go a little way to make up for such a rotten experience.

Q: Ten years ago I was convicted of a shoplifting offence – an isolated incident – for which I was fined £40. I have since remarried and I have not even told my husband about my conviction as I was so ashamed at what had happened. I am now very worried as my husband wants me to go to America with him and I understand that the visa application form requires information to be given regarding previous convictions. As this offence was so long ago, do I still have to declare it on the form, or can I consider that the slate is now wiped clean?

A: Under British law your long-ago conviction is regarded as 'spent', in other words, you are generally entitled to treat this unhappy episode as if it had never happened. However, when dealing with visa applications for a foreign land, you may well be

expected to disclose the fact of this conviction to satisfy their legal requirements. We would recommend that you write to the American Embassy for guidance on this point. They will not deal with any enquiries by phone.

Q: Please settle a dispute! I say that it is theft to remove an article from a shelf in a shop intending to take it without paying, even if you change your mind and put it back. My friend insists that the stealing only occurs when you leave the shop.

A: Your friend is wrong. What you are really faced with, however, is a problem of proof since it is far more difficult to prove that a person intends to steal if they are still within the shop. None the less, as a matter of law, if an intention to steal is formed and an article removed with that intent, the act of theft has taken place even if a change of heart follows.

Q: I was stationary at traffic lights when I was hit in the rear by a van whose driver told me that his brakes failed. My car was badly damaged and I injured my neck. However, I have now found out, through my insurers, that the van driver was uninsured. Is there any way that I can be recompensed for my injury or my losses – in particular my no-claim bonus, as this affects my premiums. The driver owned the van.

A: Any financial loss you suffer can only be recovered from the driver himself – if he is worth suing. If not, don't waste your time and money. However, there is a body called the Motor Insurers' Bureau which does cover claims where the party at fault is uninsured or disappears, and you should seek professional advice as to how to go about instituting such a claim.

Q: As I approached a pedestrian crossing I proceeded as I saw no one waiting to cross. I was almost at the crossing when a young woman rushed in front of my car. Although I braked I was unable to avoid hitting her, although fortunately she was not seriously hurt. Despite her insistence to the police that it was her fault, I have received a summons to attend the magistrates' court. I am distressed beyond words as I have always been so careful on the road.

A: Why oh why do some pedestrians think that a crossing gives them a divine right to walk (or run) in front of a moving vehicle? They forget that they do not possess divine immunity from injury if they are hit!

Although you don't say, we expect that you have been summonsed for failing to accord precedence at a pedestrian crossing. Strictly speaking, this is precisely what you did, since a pedestrian – even a kamikaze one – has an absolute right of precedence on a crossing. None the less, although you were technically at fault, we hope that the magistrate exercises sensible discretion and gives you the discharge you deserve.

Incidentally, in any civil suit by such a pedestrian claiming damages for her injuries against you, the issue of fault would be considered, and if the fault was found to be substantially or totally that of the pedestrian, as appears the case here, then it is likely she would get little or even nothing by way of compensation.

Q: Last year I was involved in a serious car accident, as a result of which I suffered multiple injuries. I was in a coma for two weeks, and after I was discharged from hospital I discovered that the police were taking no action against the other driver as there were no independent witnesses. I have now recovered from my injuries but I wondered whether there was any authority from whom I could claim compensation.

A: The fact that there were no independent witnesses does not mean that you cannot bring a claim of negligence against the other driver. It all depends on the facts of the case as to whether you would recover compensation and, of course, it would be your word against that of the other driver. However, you could pursue your claim in the court, and if you could show that there was some fault on the part of the other driver then you could at least recover damages for some of your injuries. If there is merit in your claim, you could qualify for legal aid to bring your case, and if the identity of the other driver is unknown (or he is uninsured) then you could recover damages from The Motor Insurers Bureau (MIB). Your solicitor will advise you.

Q: I was running for a bus and I'm sure the driver saw me, but he drove on. I tried to jump on but slipped and hit my knee against the railing, which put me out of action for a month. Can I sue the bus company?

A: Unfortunately, if you leap for a moving bus, on your head be it – or in this case on your knee! The fact that the bus driver may have seen you might make him inconsiderate, but it still doesn't make either him or the bus company legally liable for your efforts to crack the urban 100-metre dash.

Q: My son, aged eight, was injured at a local firework display when a catherine wheel flew off a tree and hit him. He was standing at the front of a crowd of children who had all been 'organised' into position by those responsible for the display. The organisers have refused to accept responsibility and state that the firework must have been defective. Can I seek compensation for my son, who has a nasty scar on his forehead, and if so, from whom?

A: The organisers of such a display must be aware of their responsibilities to those invited or paying to watch. If onlookers are allowed to stand too close or the fireworks are ignited into a crowd, any injury resulting is the liability of those in charge if it is shown that the incident was caused by their insufficient care in setting up the display.

If the firework was indeed defective, as is claimed here, then the supplier could be liable – although ultimate responsibility lies with the manufacturer, to whom an injured party could look for compensation.

In the first instance you should write to the organisers, setting out your complaints. If you get no joy from them, you should then get in touch with the firework's manufacturer, if you know who it was. If this all fizzles out like a damp squib, go to your local law centre or Citizens' Advice Bureau.

Q: My fifteen-year-old son has wanted to be a lawyer since he was ten, and his father and I are very keen to encourage him. Our problem is that he runs around with a gang at school who are always up to some mischief. They don't commit any serious crimes but one of the boys was caught stealing a bag of sweets and was cautioned by a police officer. If our son had been involved, how would this have affected him and his ambition?

A: Police officers do prefer to caution youngsters in these circumstances but, on the whole, it's best not to risk any kind of record, whether you want to be a barrister or a barman!

Children under the age of seventeen can only be cautioned if they admit guilt and if the parents consent. The child, accompanied by a parent, is brought before a senior police officer and given a warning that if he commits any more offences, he is likely to be taken to court. This usually has a deterring effect and we're sure your child will not wish to reach that point. A caution, however, is not a conviction and need not be disclosed as such.

APPENDIX
USEFUL ADDRESSES

There are lots of organisations ready to answer your questions. Your local library should be useful here as well as the Citizens' Advice Bureau or Law Centre. We list below some helpful addresses.

General Application

> The Law Society
> 113 Chancery Lane
> London WC2 1PA
> 01–242 1222
>
> The Law Society of Scotland
> 26 Drumsheugh Gardens
> Edinburgh EH3 7YR
> 031–226 7411
>
> The Law Society of Northern Ireland
> Law Society House
> 90 Victoria Street
> Belfast BT1 3JZ
> 0232 231614
>
> The National Council for Civil Liberties
> 21 Tabard Street
> London SE1
> 01–403 3888
>
> Rights of Women
> 52–54 Featherstone Street
> London EC1Y 8RT
> 01–251 6577

Employment

Central Office of the Industrial Tribunal
(England and Wales)
93 Ebury Bridge Road
London SW1W 8RE
01-730 9161

Central Office of the Industrial Tribunal
(Scotland)
St Andrews House
141 West Nile Street
Glasgow G1 2RU
041-331 1601

Equal Opportunities Commission
Overseas House
Quay Street
Manchester M3 3HN
061-833 9244

Advisory, Conciliation and Arbitration Service
(ACAS)
Regional offices:

(Northern Region)
Westgate House
Westgate Street
Newcastle upon Tyne NE1 1TJ
0632 612191

(Yorkshire and Humberside Region)
City House
Leeds LS1 4JH
0532 38232

(North-Western Region)
Boulton House
17-21 Chorlton Street

Manchester M1 3HY
061-228 3222

(London and South-Eastern Region)
Clifton House
83-117 Euston Road
London NW1 2RB
01-388 5100

(South-Western Region)
16 Park Place
Clifton
Bristol BS8 NP
0272 211921

(Midlands Region)
Alpha Tower
Suffolk Street
Queensway
Birmingham B1 1TZ
021-643 9911

ACAS Office for Scotland
Franborough House
123-127 Bothwell Street
Glasgow GR 7VR
041-204 2677

ACAS Office for Wales
Phase 1
Ty Glas Road
Llanishen
Cardiff CF4 5PH
0222 762636

Claims for Compensation for Criminal Injury

>Criminal Injuries Compensation Board
>19 Alfred Place
>Chenies Street
>London WC1E 7LG
>01–636 9501

>Criminal Injuries Compensation Board
>(Scotland)
>Blythswood House
>200 West Regent Street
>Glasgow G2 4SW
>041–221 0945

Claims on Road Where Driver Untraced or Uninsured

>Motor Insurers' Bureau
>(for England, Wales and Scotland)
>New Garden House
>78 Hatton Garden
>London EC1N 8JQ
>01–242 0033

Home-Buying and Mortgages

>Building Societies Association
>3 Savile Row
>London W1X 1AF
>01–437 0655

Divorce and Separation

>Marriage Guidance Council (Relate)
>76a New Cavendish Street
>London W1M 7LB
>01–580 1087

>Marriage Guidance Council (Relate)
>26 Frederick Street

Edinburgh EM2 2JR
031-225 5006

Divorce Conciliation and Advisory Service
38 Ebury Street
London SW1 WLO
01-730 2422

Catholic Marriage Advisory Council
196 Clyde Street
Glasgow G1 4JY
041-204 1239

Children

National Association for the Childless
318 Summer Lane
Birmingham B19 3RL
021-359 4887

The Children's Legal Centre
20 Compton Terrace
London N2 2UN
01-359 6251

Scottish Child Law Centre
1 Melrose Street
Glagow G4 9BJ
041-333 9305

British Agencies for Adoption and Fostering
11 Southwark Street
London SE1 1SM
01-407 8800

Violence or Crisis

Rape Crisis Centre
PO Box 69

London WC1 5BE
01-837 1600

Women's Aid Federation
(England)
52-54 Featherstone Street
London EC1Y 8RT
01-251 6537

State Benefits or Information

Disability Alliance
25 Denmark Street
London WC2 8NJ
01-240 0806

Age Concern
60 Pitcairn Road
Mitcham
Surrey CR4 3LL
01-640 5431

Scottish Council for Disablement
5 Shandwick Place
Edinburgh E82 4RG
031-229 8632

Data Information on Credit References

Westcot Data
10 Union Street
Glasgow G1 3QX

CCN Systems Limited
Talbot House
Talbot Street
Nottingham NG1 5HF
0602 419961

Infolink Limited
Coombe Cross
2/4 South End
Croydon CR0 1DL
01-686 5644

Registry Trust Limited
173-175 Cleveland Street
London W1P 5PE
01-380 0133

Director General of Fair Trading
Field House
Bream's Buildings
London EC4A 1PR
01-242 2858

MAKING A SMALL CLAIM – IT'S NO BIG DEAL

A dispute with a shopkeeper; your laundry goes missing; your car repairs are hopeless: these are, as we have seen, all examples of everyday frustrations, and if persuasion, cajoling, arguing or even correspondence have failed to bring about a satisfactory result, you can bring a claim in what is commonly called the 'small claims court', but which is actually an arbitration action in the local county court (the address can be found in the telephone directory). Any claim up to £500.00 comes within the small claims procedure.

In the preceding pages of this book we have told you when it is appropriate to apply this procedure – now here's how:

First, you present yourself at the court office and obtain a claim form for which a small fee (court fee) on a sliding scale is paid. On this form you are referred to as the plaintiff, i.e. the person making the claim. You set out your name, address, the nature of your claim, how much you are claiming and briefly why and upon what basis you say you are entitled to make your claim. You give details of the person or company from whom you wish to claim – they are referred to as the defendant. The court then sends a copy to the defendant and the action is under way.

The next step is when you and the defendant are given a date to attend court. This is called the pre-trial review, and here you will be advised on the preparation of your case. You may be told to produce photographs, a plan or an invoice, or to have an expert available for the main hearing. If the defendant fails to attend this appointment you may even get your judgment there and then.

Now the trial date is set and you go to court armed with

the facts and any evidence which you wish to produce – the spoilt garment; the A.A. report outlining the bad car repairs, any invoices and receipts, or whatever is relevant to your case. Presentation of evidence is, for the most part, informal but if you are relying on what somebody has told you, then it is best to try and get this person to court to give the evidence himself. Sometimes the court will accept a witness's evidence by signed statement, if the witness is unable to attend court. The arbitrator (normally the court registrar) will hear both sides and will give his decision. There is generally no appeal, and no costs are allowed other than expenses for attending plus the original court fee for the winning side.

That's all there is to it!

INDEX

abortion, 57–8
accident insurance, 57
adoption, 56, 68–9, 70–1
AIDS, 74
animal, pet
  injury to, 26
  see also cat; dog

'baby farm', 71
bank
  Joint account, 37
  son's debt to, 86
bigamy, 42–3
birth certificate, alteration of, virtually impossible, 60
book club, cancellation of membership, 16–17
breast cancer, investigation for, 77
builders
  estimates and charges, 14
  unsatisfactory work by, 113–14, 116, 118
  work abandoned by, 116
bungalow
  building regulations to be complied with, 109–10
  noise through party wall, 109–10
burglary
  insurers' refusal to pay, 92
  phone used by burglars, 109
bus, passenger injured on, 125, 130

car
  damaged by emergency vehicle, 126
  damaged by supermarket trolley, 123
  damaged by uninsured driver, 128
  damaged by visitors to youth club, 31–2
  driven over neighbour's lawn, 27–8
  parked in street, 114–15
  second-hand, found to be faulty, 87
  stolen, purchaser has no title to, 90–1
  see also car accident; car insurance; driving lessons; pedestrian crossing; speeding offences
car accident
  caused by dog, 61–2
  compensation for injuries, 126, 127–8
  compensation paid to widows etc., 50–1
  insurers' refusal to pay, 81–2
car insurance
  insurers' refusal to pay, 81–2, 90
  no-claim bonus, 94
carpet, wrongly taken by ex-husband, 42

cat, dispute with neighbour over, 65
caution, is not a conviction, 131–2
child, non-marital, 53
'child of the family', 57
children
  access by grandparents, 58–9
  attacked by dog, 65
  'buying' of, 70–1
  care proceedings, 62–3, 63–4
  cautioned by police, 131
  compensation on death of common-law father, 50–1
  illegitimate, 42–3, 53, 59–60
  legal liability for, assumed by father, 57
  maintenance of, *see* maintenance
  Pill prescribed for, 77
  surname change, 55, 60–1
  see also abortion; adoption; parents; school; son, grown-up
cleaner, *see* dry cleaner
clothes
  damaged by dog, 64–5
  damaged by dry cleaner, 17–18
  damaged by waiter, 26
  loan of, 26
  not kept for customer, despite agreement to do so, 10–11
  returned to shop when not faulty, 9–10
  see also washing instructions
club, *see* youth club
confidentiality, breach of, 33–34
contract of sale
  breach of, 10–11
  formation of, 14
conversation, recording of, 33
conversion (a form of theft), 42
conviction, spent, 127–8
copyright
  in letters, 33–34
  none in titles, 100
cottage, old
  defective repairs to, 118–19
  neighbouring property damaged by outbuildings, 118–19
council house, liability for injury to visitor, 112
credit, refusal of, 94–6
credit cards, debts must be settled from deceased's estate, 94
credit notes and refunds, 9–10, 15–16, 20–1, 21
credit reference agency, 94–6
crime, lateness in reporting, 125
Criminal Injuries Compensation Board, 121–2

dance floor, slippery, causing injury, 102–3

INDEX

deed of factory and commission (in Scotland), 82
delay, unreasonable, in making repairs, 13
delivery, of goods from shops etc., 14–15, 18–19
dental treatment, 74–5
disco, in residential property, 30–1
divorce
  under Islamic law, 43
  problems after, 35–6, 37–8, 38, 39, 39–40, 40–1, 42–3, 43, 46–7, 57
  unreasonable conduct as basis of, 36–7
  see also separation
doctor
  claims against, 75, 76; *see also* medical negligence
  sex of, patient cannot insist on, 78
  see also hospital; medical records; medical reports; surgery
dog
  back door damaged by, 26–7
  car accident caused by, 61–2
  children attacked by, 65
  clothes damaged by, 64–5
  control orders on, 26–7, 32
  dangerous, 32, 65
  dispute with neighbours over, 27–8
  pet animal injured by, 27
driving lessons, theft by instructor, 19–20
dry cleaner, damage done by, 17–18

education, *see* school
emergency vehicles, and traffic lights, 126
employee, dishonest, employer's responsibility for behaviour of, 19–20
Employers' Liability (Defective Equipment) Act 1969, 101
employment, *see* work
estate agents
  commission due if purchaser obtained through, 17
  damage caused by sign, 113–4
  particulars supplied by, 110–111
estimate, builder's refusal to abide by, 14
extension, left incomplete by builder, 116

fence, damaged by tree-felling, 29
firework display, injury sustained at, 130–1
flat
  disposal of, after divorce, 45–6
  let during absence abroad, 113
  live-in lovers and, 49–50

purchase 'subject to contract', 107
sale of, money due on completion, 84
too small for furniture, 110–11
see also flat, rented; house

flat, rented
eviction from, 83–4, 115
joint tenancy, 83–4
landlord's neglect of repairs, 119–20
licence to occupy, does not give security of tenure, 83–4
licence or tenancy, 116–17
sitting tenant, purchase by, 85–6
tenants' right to buy when landlord sells, 108

freezer, defective, food ruined by, 11
friends, letters written to, 33–4
fruit, on overhanging branches of neighbour's tree, 31
furniture, delay in delivery of, 18–19

gazumping, 107
'goodwill' payment by shop, 11
grandparents
access to grandchildren, 58–9
in care proceedings, 62–3
Gretna Green, 47–8
Guard Dogs Act 1975, 32–3

hairdresser, mistake by, 10
harassment
by ex-boyfriend, 51
by neighbours, 28–9

holidays
expenses, disagreement after sharing of, 51–2
expenses, unexpected, incurred, 21–2
non-arrival of luggage, 126–7
from school, in term-time, 62

hospital, negligence by, 73–4
hotel, liable for negligence of staff, 25

house
accidental injury to visitor, 112
damaged by tree, 117–8
disco held in, 30–1
after divorce, 37–8, 38, 40, 43–4, 44
furniture and fittings, on purchase, 106–7
improvement grant, poor work done under, 113
joint tenancy, purchased as, 52
live-in lovers and, 49, 51, 51–2, 93–4
mortgage interest relief, 96
parking outside, 114–5
son's licence to occupy, 62
squatters in, 29
surveyor negligent, 114

INDEX

trees to be protected on
  sale, 117
willed to children of
  previous marriage, 39
see also bungalow; cottage;
  council house; estate
  agents; extension; flat;
  household insurance;
  neighbours; trespass
household insurance
  damage caused by dog,
    61–2
  new-for-old, 108–9
  insurers' refusal to pay, 92
  'underinsured', 92
husbands (*see also* divorce;
    marriage; wives)
  intestacy of, 84–5

income tax
  nanny's pay not a tax
    allowance, 105
  self-employed people,
    99–100
industrial tribunal, time limit
  for application to,
  100–1
inheritance
  legitimate and illegitimate
    children treated alike,
    42–3, 60
  see also intestacy; will
Inheritance (Provision for
  Family and
  Dependants) Act 1975,
  88
injury
  due to bus lurching,
    125–6
  when running for a bus,
    130
  caused by car driver,
    compensation for, 128,
    129–30
  criminal, compensation
    for, 121–22
  on dance floor, 102–3
  at firework display,
    130–31
  at school, 57, 61
  to visitor, 112
  at work, 102
insurance
  against accidents at
    school, 57
  disclosure of facts on
    proposal form, 81–2,
    91–2
  see also car insurance;
    household insurance;
    life insurance
insurance broker, wrong
  advice from, 92
intestacy
  of bachelor with brothers
    and sisters, 89
  gifts before death not part
    of estate, 80–1
  of husband, 84–5
  of parent of illegitimate
    child, 60
Islam, *see* Muslim

journalist, remarks quoted
  by, 33

knitting pattern, condition
  attached to sale of,
  13–14

INDEX

Landlord and Tenant Act 1987, 108
lawn, damaged by neighbour's car, 27–8
lawyer, *see* solicitor
legal aid, 22
letters, use of, by recipient, 33–4
life insurance, medical report for, 78–9
loan, repaid as lump sum or by instalments, 51–2
local authority
  improvement grant, poor work done under, 113
  obligation to maintain let properties, 112
lovers, live-in, 49–54, 93–4
luggage, non-arrival of, on holiday, 126–7

mail-order company, goods not sent by, 88–9
maintenance, of children
  in case of bigamy, 42–3
  after divorce, 38, 41–2, 43–4, 44–5, 57
  of unmarried parents, 53–4, 59–60, 63–4
maintenance, of wives
  in case of bigamy, 42–3
  after divorce or separation, 38–9, 41–2, 48
manufacturer, shopkeeper cannot pass responsibility to, 20–1
markets, defective goods purchased at, 21
marriage
  bigamous, 42–3, 43
  at Gretna Green, 47
  of minors, 47
  prohibited between relations, 46–7
  purification in mosque not recognised as, 43
  tax relief on mortgage, 96
  teenage father's reluctance, 63–4
  video-recording of, 39–40
  wife taking husband's name, 37
  to witness of will, 85
  see also divorce; separation; wives
mastectomy, 77
maternity leave and pay, 103–4, 105
medical negligence, 73, 76
medical records, patients' access to, 72–3, 75
medical reports, patients' access to, 78–9
meter readers, impersonation of, 122
minors, marriage of, 47–8
molestation, by husband, 36–7
money, retention of, without entitlement, 84
mortgage, tax relief on, 96
Motor Insurers' Bureau, 128, 130
mugging, 121–22
music, loud, 24–5
musical instruments, unfit for purpose, 20
Muslims, Islamic law,

INDEX

purification ceremony
  in mosque, 43

name
  change of, by deed poll,
    60–61
  see also surname
nanny, her pay not a tax
  allowance, 105
national insurance
  contributions ('stamp'),
    99–100
neighbours
  complaints by, 25–6,
    27–8, 118–19
  damage caused by, 25–6,
    26–7, 28
  dangerous dogs owned by,
    32–3
  noise from, 24–5, 30–31
  overhanging trees and
    plants, 25, 30, 31
  remarks about, to
    journalist, 33
  trespass by, 26–7, 65
newspapers
  letters published by, 33–4
  remarks quoted by, 33
no-claim bonus, 94
noise
  made by neighbours,
    24–5, 30–1
  through party wall,
    109–10

old people, problems with,
  82–3
operation, unsatisfactory,
  75–6
organist, performing rights
  in wedding video-
    recording, 39–40

parents
  not responsible for son's
    debts, 86
  unpleasant behaviour by
    son, 62
  see also children;
    surrogacy
paternity test, 53–4, 63–4
pay packet, error in, 84
pedestrian crossing, 129
performing rights, of
  organist in wedding
    video, 39–40
Pill, prescribed for children,
  77
planning permission, 30–1
police
  children cautioned by,
    131–2
  impersonation of, 122
pools syndicate, 81
possessions, household
  after divorce, 40–1, 45–6
  live-in lovers and, 49–50
possessions, personal,
  wrongly taken by ex-
    wife, 40–41
power of attorney, 82–3
property, *see* flat *and* house;
  or possessions

rabbit, pet, savaged by dog,
  26
rape
  in marriage, 36
  not reported by victim,
    125

INDEX

recording device, *see* tape-recording
repairs, not done or done badly, 13, 15, 19
restaurants, poor food or service in, 22–3
retirement age, for women, 103
Rottweilers, 32
rugby football, accidental injury due to, 57

Salvation Army, can help trace parents, 56
school
  accidental injury at, 57, 61
  divorced parents' disagreement over, 36–7
  holidays taken in term-time, 62
  mixed-ability classes and streaming, 66–7
  reasonable supervision, lack of, 61
  religious instruction in, 66
self-employed people, 99–100, 105
sentences, in court, variability of, 123
separation
  distribution of property after, 37–8, 42, 44–5
  grandparents and care proceedings, 62–3
  see also divorce
service charges, in restaurants, 22–3
sexual discrimination, at work, 97

sexual harassment, at work, 97–8
shoplifting
  conviction spent, 127–8
  intention to steal is theft, 128
  suspected, 12–13
shops, stores, supermarkets
  conditions of sale imposed by, 13–14
  credit notes or refunds from, 9–10, 15–16, 20–1, 21
  customer defaulting on payment, 16
  customer's bag searched, 12–13
  delivery arrangements, 14–15
  goods defective, 20–1, 21
  goods not kept for customer, despite agreement to do so, 10–11
  'goodwill' payment by, 11
  intention to steal from, 128
  liability not passed back to manufacturer, 20–1
  liability wrongly denied by, 17–18
'small claims' procedure, 141
  some examples of use of, 15, 18, 20, 29, 101, 110, 137
smear tests
  repeat of, 76
  wrong diagnosis from, 76
smoking, banned at work, 98–9

INDEX

solicitor
  advice when choosing, 12, 73–4
  change of, 11–12, 22
  complaints against, 11–12, 73, 84
  payment of, when dissatisfied, 11–12
son, grown-up
  parents not responsible for debts, 86
  unpleasantness at home, 62
speeding offences, variability of fines for, 122–3
squatters, 29
stall holders, liability of, no different from shopkeeper's, 21
stamp, national insurance, 99
stores, *see* shops
supermarkets
  damage caused by trolleys, 123
  see also shops
surgery
  consent to, 77–8
  unsatisfactory, 75–6
surname
  of child, change of, 55, 60–1
  choice of, by married couple, 37
surrogacy, 68–9, 70 (twice)

tape recording
  as evidence in court, 59–60
  can be made secretly, 33

taxation (of solicitor's bill), 12
telephone
  large bill after burglar's use of phone, 109
  obscene calls, 111
television, repairs to, unsatisfactory or not done, 15, 19
tenancy, tenant, *see* flat, rented
theft, some forms of, 19–20, 42, 84, 127
tour operators, complaints about, 21–2, 126–7
traffic lights, emergency vehicles and, 126
transfer of property orders, 50
travel agents, 21–2
trees
  damage caused when felling, 29
  damage caused by roots, 117–8
  preservation orders, 117
trees and plants
  overhanging, 25, 30, 31
  preservation of, when moving house, 117
trespass, 26–7, 65
trial, delay in fixing date of, 22

undue influence, 81, 88
Unfair Contract Terms Act 1977, 18
unfair dismissal, *see under* work

upholsterer, unreasonable
delay by, 13

video-recording, performing
rights concerning,
39–40

visa application, information
regarding convictions,
127–8

wages, outstanding, refusal
to pay, 100–101
waiter, food spilt on clothes
by, 25
washing instructions,
incorrect, damage due
to, 20–1, 21
weapons, offensive
illegal to carry, 124
may be used in self-
defence, 124
will
of adopted child's natural
father, 56
advisability of making, 84–5,
89
alterations to, 86–7, 91–2
beneficiary does not lose by
subsequent marriage to
witness, 85
challenge to, 39, 88, 93–4
children of previous
marriage, provision for,
39
essential requirements of,
91–2

executors, 91
to make your own, 91–2
no will made, *see* intestacy
undue influence over, 88
witnesses, must witness
signatures, 91
wives
compensation payment on
death of common-law
husband, 50–51
maintenance of, *see*
maintenance
contested by husband,
36–7
see also divorce; marriage
women, self-defence against
attack, 122, 124, 125
work
injury at, 102
notice, entitlement to, 99
part-time employee,
rights of, 101, 103–4
retirement age, for
women, 103
sexual discrimination at,
98
sexual harassment at,
97–98
smoking ban, 98–99
unfair dismissal, 98–99,
99–100, 100–1, 102
see also maternity leave
writer's circle, 100

youth club, nuisance from,
31–2

Bestselling Non-Fiction

☐ Complete Hip and Thigh Diet	Rosemary Conley	£2.99
☐ Staying off the Beaten Track	Elizabeth Gundrey	£6.99
☐ Raw Energy: Recipes	Leslie Kenton	£3.99
☐ The PM System	Dr J A Muir Gray	£5.99
☐ Women Who Love Too Much	Robin Norwood	£3.50
☐ Letters From Women Who Love Too Much	Robin Norwood	£3.50
☐ Fat is a Feminist Issue	Susie Orbach	£2.99
☐ Callanetics	Callan Pinckney	£6.99
☐ Elvis and Me	Priscilla Presley	£3.50
☐ Love, Medicine and Miracles	Bernie Siegel	£3.50
☐ Communion	Whitley Strieber	£3.50
☐ Trump: The Art of the Deal	Donald Trump	£3.99

Prices and other details are liable to change

ARROW BOOKS, BOOKSERVICE BY POST, PO BOX 29, DOUGLAS, ISLE OF MAN, BRITISH ISLES

NAME..

ADDRESS...

....

....

Please enclose a cheque or postal order made out to Arrow Books Ltd. for the amount due and allow the following for postage and packing.

U.K. CUSTOMERS: Please allow 22p per book to a maximum of £3.00.

B.F.P.O. & EIRE: Please allow 22p per book to a maximum of £3.00.

OVERSEAS CUSTOMERS: Please allow 22p per book.

Whilst every effort is made to keep prices low it is sometimes necessary to increase cover prices at short notice. Arrow Books reserve the right to show new retail prices on covers which may differ from those previously advertised in the text or elsewhere.

A Selection of Arrow Books

☐	No Enemy But Time	Evelyn Anthony	£2.95
☐	The Lilac Bus	Maeve Binchy	£2.99
☐	Rates of Exchange	Malcolm Bradbury	£3.50
☐	Prime Time	Joan Collins	£3.50
☐	Rosemary Conley's Complete Hip and Thigh Diet	Rosemary Conley	£2.99
☐	Staying Off the Beaten Track	Elizabeth Gundrey	£6.99
☐	Duncton Wood	William Horwood	£4.50
☐	Duncton Quest	William Horwood	£4.50
☐	A World Apart	Marie Joseph	£3.50
☐	Erin's Child	Sheelagh Kelly	£3.99
☐	Colours Aloft	Alexander Kent	£2.99
☐	Gondar	Nicholas Luard	£4.50
☐	The Ladies of Missalonghi	Colleen McCullough	£2.50
☐	The Veiled One	Ruth Rendell	£3.50
☐	Sarum	Edward Rutherfurd	£4.99
☐	Communion	Whitley Strieber	£3.99

Prices and other details are liable to change

ARROW BOOKS, BOOKSERVICE BY POST, PO BOX 29, DOUGLAS, ISLE OF MAN, BRITISH ISLES

NAME...

ADDRESS...

....

....

Please enclose a cheque or postal order made out to Arrow Books Ltd. for the amount due and allow the following for postage and packing.

U.K. CUSTOMERS: Please allow 22p per book to a maximum of £3.00.

B.F.P.O. & EIRE: Please allow 22p per book to a maximum of £3.00.

OVERSEAS CUSTOMERS: Please allow 22p per book.

Whilst every effort is made to keep prices low it is sometimes necessary to increase cover prices at short notice. Arrow Books reserve the right to show new retail prices on covers which may differ from those previously advertised in the text or elsewhere.

Arrow Health

☐ The Alexander Principle	Wilfred Barlow	£2.95
☐ The Zinc Solution	D. Bryce-Smith	£3.50
☐ Goodbye to Arthritis	Patricia Byrivers	£2.95
☐ Rosemary Conley's Complete Hip and Thigh Diet	Rosemary Conley	£2.99
☐ No Change	Wendy Cooper	£2.99
☐ Day Light Robbery	Dr Damien Downing	£3.99
☐ The Biogenic Diet	Leslie Kenton	£3.99
☐ Ageless Ageing: The Natural Way to Stay Young	Leslie Kenton	£3.95
☐ Raw Energy: Recipes	Leslie Kenton	£3.99
☐ Joy of Beauty	Leslie Kenton	£6.99
☐ Sexual Cystitis	Angela Kilmartin	£3.99
☐ PM System: Preventive Medicine For Total Health	Dr JA Muir Gray	£5.99
☐ Women Who Love Too Much	Robin Norwood	£3.50
☐ Fat is a Feminist Issue	Susie Orbach	£2.99
☐ Callanetics	Callan Pinckney	£6.99
☐ Love, Medicine and Miracles	Bernie Siegel	£3.50

Prices and other details are liable to change

ARROW BOOKS, BOOKSERVICE BY POST, PO BOX 29, DOUGLAS, ISLE OF MAN, BRITISH ISLES

NAME...

ADDRESS..

....

....

Please enclose a cheque or postal order made out to Arrow Books Ltd. for the amount due and allow the following for postage and packing.

U.K. CUSTOMERS: Please allow 22p per book to a maximum of £3.00.

B.F.P.O. & EIRE: Please allow 22p per book to a maximum of £3.00.

OVERSEAS CUSTOMERS: Please allow 22p per book.

Whilst every effort is made to keep prices low it is sometimes necessary to increase cover prices at short notice. Arrow Books reserve the right to show new retail prices on covers which may differ from those previously advertised in the text or elsewhere.